BATMAN, ROBIN, DAVID BECKHAM AND THE NAKED KING

The Definitive Guide to Becoming a Better Presenter

TAB EDWARDS

TMBE, PHILADELPHIA, PA 19129

TMBE PHILADELPHIA, PA

ISBN 978-0-9700891-5-1

This publication is designed to provide authoritative information in regards to the subject matter covered. It is sold with the understanding that the publisher is not engaged in rendering legal, accounting, or other professional services. If legal advice or other expert assistance is required, the services of a competent professional person should be sought.

—From a declaration of principles jointly adopted by a committee of the American Bar Association and a committee of publishers.

Tab Edwards books are available at special quantity discounts to use as premiums and promotions, or for use in corporate training programs. For more information, please visit the website TabEdwards.com.

Designed by Joshua Black of Blackeyesoup.com
Philadelphia, PA.

1   3   5   7   9   10   8   6   4   2

To Jaylo, Sabrina, Germaine,
Butter and Puddie

CONTENTS

PART SIX
Fine-Tuning 153

BATMAN, ROBIN, DAVID BECKHAM AND THE NAKED KING

The Definitive Guide to Becoming a Better Presenter

TAB EDWARDS

" When delivering a speech or presentation, either know of what you speak and show, or DON'T."

—Tab Edwards

Author, *Lessons of the Navel Orange*

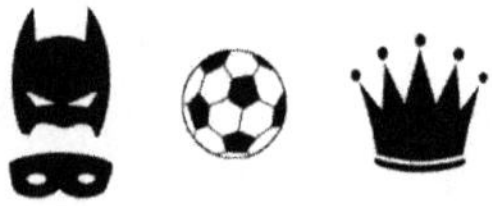

Introduction

Batman, Robin, David Beckham, and the Naked King

Overcoming the most fallacious teachings about "good" presentations

Far too many people are under the impression that great presentations are based on fancy PowerPoint slides, slick integrated video, a smooth presentation style, and the seductive appeal of the presenter. Sadly, this impression is erroneous. The best presentations are those that are based on strong *content*, and, as I will make the argument throughout this book, everything else is secondary.

When people attend presentations, what is the *primary* reason why they do so? To see fancy PowerPoint slides? No. To see a slick video? No. To witness a smooth presenter in action? No? To hear and see the presenter—regardless of what that presenter will be presenting? No. The primary reason why most people attend presentations is the *content* or *topics* that are being discussed; and as a presenter, it is important to understand this critical point as you prepare for your presentations.

Skeptics will argue that the *person* delivering the presentation is just as influential a reason why people attend presentations as is the *content* of a presentation. They argue, for example, that if Oprah Winfrey or some other A-List celebrity was giving a presentation, people would attend the presentation because of the presenter's *celebrity*. I will concede that there are some occasions when a person will attend a presentation—regardless of the topic being discussed—just to go see the *person*. In such cases, is the person attending the presentation on the merits of the presentation, or is the person attending the presentation to see the presenter—regardless of the topic being discussed? If the reason is the latter, then you cannot say that the person is "attending the presentation." Instead, you must say that they are "going to see a celebrity; there is a difference.

It's like going to a restaurant. Fundamentally, why do you go to a restaurant? To eat food. So the food (the "content") is the primary reason why you go to a restaurant. If Oprah Winfrey was to make an appearance at a restaurant—but no food is to be served—and you decided to go anyway just to see Oprah, then would you be going to the restaurant for the primary function of the restaurant (food)? No. And if Oprah changed her mind and decided to appear at the local college, would you still go to the restaurant? No. So in the end, you wouldn't be "going to the restaurant," but instead, you would be "going to see Oprah."

So I ask: In such cases, is the person's primary reason for attending the presentation the *presentation* (the food) or the *presenter* (Oprah)? In the Oprah Winfrey example, the person would be going to see the *presenter* (Oprah Winfrey) and NOT the *presentation*. Therefore, my contention holds true that people primarily attend presentations (the restaurant) based on the presentation's content (the food). In a restaurant, the food is king. In a presentation, the *content is king*.

Consider this: Bobby West is an Iowa vegetable farmer who is interested in learning new techniques for maximizing the yield of his vegetable harvest. On Friday evening there will be two presentations held in Bob's small town: one presentation will be delivered by Sam Gordon, a local farmer who has found a way to increase the yield of his vegetable crops five-fold; the other presentation will be a star-studded affair featuring Oprah Winfrey, Julia Roberts, football player Peyton Manning, and singer Bono. These celebrities will be delivering presentations explaining the most humane ways of raising and butchering pigs.

If you were Bobby West, which presentation would you attend? There is no way imaginable that ol' farmer Sam Gordon can match the star power of the presenters at the competing presentation. Yet—because of the *content* of each presentation—the smart money says that Bobby West would attend Sam's presentation where the content is related to an issue that Bobby is genuinely interested in learning about. (See the table below). In this and in most cases, *content trumps celebrity*!

Presentation Options

Background Information	Sam Gordon	Oprah, Julia, Peyton, Bono
Topic of the Presentation ➤	How I Increased the Yield of my Vegetable Crops Five Fold	The Most Humane Ways of Raising and Butchering Pigs
Bob's Goal for Attending the Presentation: To learn new techniques for maximizing the yield the yield of his vegetable ➤	Relevant	Irrelevant
Alignment between Bob's goal and the presentation topic ➤	Strong	Weak
Likelihood of Bob attending this presentation ➤	High	Low

The Three-Part Proposition

The best presentations are those which adhere to the following *Three-Part Proposition*:

Part 1: The most effective presentations are based on clearly-articulated **goals**. These goals are supported by clearly-defined objectives and desired presentation outcomes.

Part 2: The most effective presentations are based on relevant **content** that supports the presentation's goals, objectives, and desired outcomes. In this sense, the *content is king*!

Part 3: The most effective communication vehicles (such as presentation slides using Microsoft PowerPoint and OpenOffice Impress) are those that are **simple and supportive**; they should not steal the audience's attention away from the presenter.

Taking this simple three-part concepts into consideration—and executing them as you develop and deliver your presentations—can immediately improve the quality of your presentations, even if your name is not *Oprah*!

To help you keep these ideas top-of-mind and to overcome the fallacious presentation teachings you may have learned in the past, I have created this simple model as a memory-jogger.

- Part 1. Goal: **David Beckham**
- Part 2. Content is **King**
- Part 3. Supporting Tools: Robin (from **Batman & Robin**)

The Three Part Proposition

1	GOAL	David Beckham	David Beckham scores soccer **goals**. Goals establish the reasons why the presentation is being conducted. You must define a goal for the presentation. Every aspect of the presentation should be directed toward the achievement of the goal.
2	CONTENT	The King	In a presentation, Content is **KING!** People attend presentations based on the content and topics being presented. Presentation content should be developed and delivered in support of the established **Goals** for the presentation.
3	SUPPORT TOOLS	Batman & Robin	Presentation slides should be the **Robin to you as Batman**. Slides should support you when and as needed; they should not detract from you and should remain unobtrusive until called upon. And remember, when developing slides, follow my KEN Principle: KEEP 'EM NAKED! Slides should be mimimalist and simple.

Admittedly, as you will read throughout this book, these three concepts are not the only elements of an effective presentation. For instance, presentation **delivery** (communication effectiveness, style, poise, etc.) can have a significant impact on the goodness and effectiveness of a presentation. The reason why presentation delivery is not included in my Three-Part Proposition is because—unlike goals, content, and a presentation's supporting tools —presentation delivery prowess cannot be executed *immediately* as can these three elements. A presenter's delivery effectiveness takes practice and time to improve upon. But as you can see in the diagram below, it is quite important in the overall scheme of an effective presentation.

PRESENTATION INTERRELATIONSHIPS

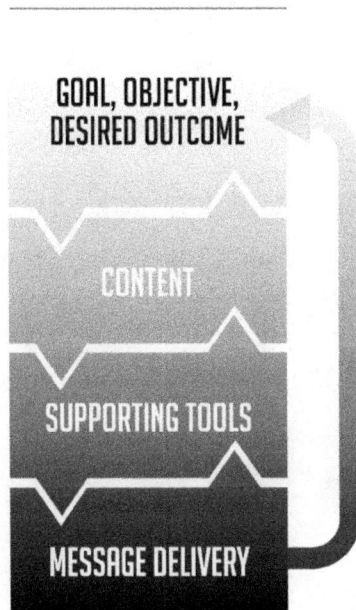

GOAL, OBJECTIVE, DESIRED OUTCOME

CONTENT

SUPPORTING TOOLS

MESSAGE DELIVERY

No, the three elements of my proposition are not the only things that can improve the effectiveness of a presentation, but they are three of—if not *the*—most important things that you can do *immediately* that will have the greatest impact on improving the overall quality of your presentations.

PART ONE

What Does it All Mean?

CH 1

Speech vs. Presentation

Public speaking—as its name implies—is the act of speaking to an audience of people, often in a public forum, following a structured format and /or a set of accepted and expected protocols. Both *speeches* and *presentations* are forms of *public speaking*. This begs the question: What is the difference between a speech and a presentation? Is there a difference or is it just a matter of semantics?

Speech

As I consider it, a *speech* typically embodies the following characteristics:

- It is memorized and/or read verbatim when being delivered by the speaker.

- The speaker uses index cards or other written notes containing the speech's content as he or she relates that content—often verbatim.

- It is commonly delivered by a speaker who stands behind a podium or lectern.

- Its purpose can be to inform (most common), persuade, or motivate (least common. It is difficult to motivate or inspire an audience by reading or delivering a memorized or verbatim speech).

- It is most often delivered in a forum that is formal and not interactive.

To put it into perspective, some examples of *speeches* include: *The State of the Union* address delivered by the President of the United States, and a *Valedictory* given by a school's class valedictorian.

Presentation

A *presentation*, as I consider it, has the following characteristics:

- It is commonly delivered with the speaker standing away from a podium or lectern.

- Its purpose can be to inform, persuade (most common in business), motivate, or demonstrate.

- It is delivered with the use of visual aids such as PowerPoint slides, flip charts, and/or whiteboards.

- Although the setting can be formal, presentations are usually delivered in a less formal setting where the presenter roams a stage or room and is more animated or casual in her or his delivery.

- It is usually delivered without the use of index cards or written notes; the slides or other supporting media serve as the content guide for the speaker.

- It is delivered in a forum that is interactive.

Some examples of *presentations* include: the sales pitch delivered by sales professionals to close a deal; talks delivered by motivational speakers; and How-to instructional presentations.

Although this book and its content can help the reader craft and deliver more effective *speeches* and become a better public speaker, the primary focus of the book is on helping the reader create and deliver more effective *presentations* and, in the process, become a better presenter.

Good? Effective? Successful?

What exactly *is* a "good," "effective," or "successful" presentation? Is it one that entertains the audience? Is it one in which the presenter memorizes and flawlessly recites each written word of his or her speaker notes? Is it a presentation that the presenter delivers smoothly and with poise, showing no signs of nervousness? A more fundamental question is: Have you ever *thought about* what constitutes a "good" presentation? In my research, I have found that most people have not.

Whenever I deliver a Presentation Skills Training workshop, I ask the participants for their opinions on what makes for a "good" presentation. The answers I typically receive include such things as:

- A presentation that keeps my attention
- One in which the presenter is smooth and polished

- One that makes me laugh

- And even ... one that uses great PowerPoint slides!

Such responses are not surprising since a person's perception of the goodness of a presentation can be personal, but they are, nonetheless, generally incorrect.

Presentations are intended to serve one or more of four purposes:

- **Inform.** To make the audience aware of something; to communicate information with the intent to educate the audience; to share information that the audience will find to be interesting and of value.

- **Motivate.** To energize, inspire, or move the audience to take an action; to increase the audience's interest in engaging or reengaging in something; to entertain the audience.

- **Persuade.** To urge the audience to follow a certain or desired course of action; to convince the audience that a certain course of action is favorable to another; to influence the audience's way of thinking about or believing something.

- **Demonstrate.** To provide the audience with an understanding of how something works; to show the audience how to perform an act or use something.

A presentation is a form of *communication*. Depending on the purpose of the presentation, it can be argued that a presentation is a form of *Marketing Communication*. And Marketing Communication involves (and can even be considered a form of) *promotion*.

Promotion is defined as the coordination of all of an organization's efforts to *inform* and *persuade* an audience in an effort to sell something or promote an idea. These goals are consistent with the purposes of a presentation and are effectively accomplished through person-to-person communication—such as a presentation.

So, if the purpose of a presentation is to either inform, motivate, persuade, or demonstrate, and since a presentation is a form of promotion, and the purpose of promotion—like a presentation—is to inform and persuade, then it stands to reason that a "good" presentation is one that accomplishes its desired purpose, specifically to inform the audience of something important or to persuade the audience to follow a certain or desired course of action. Even a motivational presentation or a demonstrative presentation can have as its purpose to inform and persuade an audience.

This is not to say that motivational and demonstrative presentations themselves don't support their own purposes; they do. But, in the end, these presentations ultimately strive to persuade (to urge the audience to follow a certain or desired course of action) and to inform (to communicate information with the intent to educate the audience).

"Good" Presentations

A presenter is considered to have delivered a "good," "effective," or "successful" presentation if he or she successfully accomplishes the purpose, goal, objectives, or desired outcome of the presentation from the perspective of the audience and that of the presenter her or himself.

This begs the question: How does a presenter go about delivering a good, effective, or successful presentation? As I hope to demonstrate throughout this book, in my experience, the most important determinant of a good or successful presentation is the degree to which the presentation aligns with and satisfies both the audience's purpose for participating in the presentation and the presenter's purpose for delivering the presentation. And the primary factor in accomplishing this goal is the relevance of the presentation's *content* and the seller's ability to make the audience absorb the content's message.

One somewhat popular notion that exists in the field of presentation skills training is that "according to research," the most important and valuable aspect of a business presentation is HOW the presenter presents, and the least important is WHAT is being presented. In my experience and opinion, this is absolutely incorrect.

Here is a simple test to show how erroneous this "research" is: Assume that you own a business and that you hired a marketing firm to create a television commercial that will generate sales of your new product. Now assume that the marketing firm created two different commercials to run in two different markets: one commercial features a handsome, polished, stylish, smooth-talking actor whose presentation style is flawless but he does a poor job of conveying the value of your product. This commercial runs for one week and generates $3,000 in sales for your product.

Unlike this first commercial, the second commercial features a frumpy, unappealing actor who doesn't speak very well and whose presentation style is very annoying.

However, this actor does a great job of getting the audience to realize the value or your product. As a result, this commercial generates $10,000 in sales for your new product. The question is: which commercial would you consider to be the "best" and the most successful? Which commercial would you want to continue running? The rational person would conclude that the second commercial—the one delivered by the annoying, frumpy, inarticulate actor—is the "best" and the most successful because it did the best job of exploiting the content and accomplishing your objective to generate sales for your new product ($10,000 vs. $3,000 for commercial #1). In the end, the rational person would want to continue running the second commercial—even though the presenter's style was awful and very much inferior to the presenter's in commercial #1. And if this is the case, you have to acknowledge that the *content* (the "WHAT") more so than the presenter's *style* (the "HOW") is ultimately the most important aspect of a presentation.

Here's an even easier way to illustrate the point: Let's say that you are a William Shakespeare fan and that you purchased a ticket to attend a seminar on the topic of "Newly-discovered secrets about William Shakespeare." You show up for the seminar, take your seat, and the presenter emerges. She is poised, stylish, very articulate, and a polished presenter whose presentation style is nothing short of captivating. She opens by stating, "We have unearthed a heretofore unknown secret about William Shakespeare! He had a seventy-year-old maid who worked for him for 25 years!" The speaker then spent the next hour talking about the life of Shakespeare's secret *maid*—but she did so wonderfully!

Now assume that, a week, later, you purchased a ticket to attend a seminar titled "Newly-discovered secrets of William Shakespeare ... really!" You show up for the seminar, take your seat, and the presenter emerges. He is dreadfully boring and he speaks in a babbling monotone reminiscent of Dustin Hoffman's character Raymond "Ray" Babbitt in the 1988 film *Rain Man*. But when the speaker begins his presentation, he shares one hour's worth of well-researched, heretofore unknown, juicy facts and information about William Shakespeare that leave you wanting to hear more. The question is: which seminar would you consider to be the "best"—the one with the ultra-smooth presenter whose content was lacking or the seminar presented by Rain Man, whose content satisfied your reason for attending the seminar?

In the end, the content is King, and the presenter's job is to serve as a vehicle for communicating the content toward the purpose, goals, and objectives of the presentation. The presenter's job is not to *BE* the content but to effectively communicate it.

CH 2

Heights, Flights, and ... Public Speaking?

As described in the previous chapter, *public speaking* is the act of speaking to an audience of people. According to the National Institute of Mental Health, 74% of people have a fear of public speaking—an anxiety known as *glossophobia*. This statistic is consistent with the adage that one of the major fears people have is public speaking, right up there with a fear of snakes, heights, and flying. And when we experience such fear we get anxious, and when we get anxious our bodies are conditioned to respond in a defensive manner by increasing adrenaline secretion which produces such symptoms as increased perspiration, dry mouth, and difficulty speaking. Sound familiar? Believe it or not, these bodily reactions have a way of reducing the level of anxiety in the speaker, so when it happens to you, don't ... *sweat* it.

Why We Fear Public Speaking

Why do we experience glossophobia? Why does public speaking make us so nervous and anxious? First, let me make the point that it's okay to be nervous prior to or during a speech or presentation. Every good presenter whom I have ever known admits to being nervous prior to delivering a speech or presentation. I, too, still get nervous before taking the stage to deliver a presentation, and I have been delivering speeches and presentations on major stages for many years.

As with any other problem or challenge, if we can identify the causes of our speaker anxiety then we can begin to address the causes and, hopefully, improve our effectiveness at public speaking.

Over the twenty-plus years that I have been working with people on becoming more effective public speakers and delivering more effective presentations, I have found that the primary reasons people fear (or at least become uncomfortable with) public speaking include:

- The potential for failure by delivering a "bad" presentation or giving a "bad" speech

- Having everyone in the audience passing judgment on your performance

- Sharing information that the audience may believe to be incorrect or know to be incorrect

- Being the focal point and the center of attention before a group of strangers

If these are the primary contributors to our fear of

public speaking—fears that negatively impact our ability to deliver the most effective talk possible—then addressing each of these fears should lead us to delivering "better," more effective speeches and presentations. This is illustrated in the table below.

The Fear of Public Speaking

Reasons We Fear Public Speaking	Affects	Addressed?	Improved Speech/ Presentation?
The potential for failure by delivering a "bad" presentation or giving a "bad" speech	Delivery Style	Yes	Yes
Having everyone in the audience passing judgment on your performance	Delivery Style	Yes	Yes
Sharing information that the audience may believe or know to be incorrect	Delivery Style	Yes	Yes
Being the focal point and the center of attention before a group of strangers	Delivery Style	Yes	Yes

The aforementioned fears of public speaking have an impact on our delivery of the presentation—our presentation *style*. When we experience public speaking anxiety, our bodies respond by exhibiting such symptoms as increased perspiration, dry mouth, and difficulty speaking. During a speech or presentation, these symptoms manifest themselves as *detractors*—making the audience focus on something other than *you*, your message, or the content of your talk. These detractors often include:

- Sweating

- Dry mouth

- Shaking hands

- Stuttering

- Forgetfulness

- Lack of focus on what you are doing

- Exhibiting a lack of confidence, thus affecting the speaker's credibility

As you will learn throughout this book, the *style* with which we deliver a speech or presentation is only one element of those which make for effective speeches and presentations. And ultimately, presentation *style* is not the most important element of an effective presentation; the most important element is the *content*. So, even if you fail to address the reasons that make you fearful of giving a speech or presentation, you can take comfort in knowing that all would not be lost with your talk if your presentation content is supportive of the purpose, goals, and objectives of the presentation.

Sure, the speech or presentation may not be delivered as smoothly or gracefully as you would like, but if you can manage to effectively convey the *content* of your speech or presentation, there is a good chance that, in the end, your talk could be considered a "success" even if you are overcome by speaking anxiety.

So how does one confront and ease glossophobia or public speaking anxiety? How does one improve his or her presentation delivery skills? How does one deliver more meaningful presentations? And, most importantly, how does one become an overall better presenter? The answers to these questions and more lay in the pages ahead.

CH 3

Where's the Forest?

The saying "She couldn't see the forest for the trees" is offered to say that a person couldn't or didn't see, or couldn't appreciate the big picture of something because she was focused on the details or minutia. When this occurs by audience members during a presentation, the result is one of two likely outcomes:

A. Good for the presenter, bad for the audience

B. Bad for the presenter, bad for the audience

It could be *good for the presenter and bad for the audience* if the audience members spend the entire presentation focused on how incredibly charming, engaging, and entertaining the presenter is, while failing to absorb and comprehend the value of the message that the presenter is trying to convey. In such a case, the audience members would surely rate the presenter (and even the presentation) highly, even though the audience members failed to comprehend the message that the presentation was provided to convey. In the end, the presentation would turn out to have been *good for the presenter* (because he or she received high feedback scores) and *bad for the audience* (because they didn't comprehend and absorb the information they attended the presentation to receive).

More than once in my career, I have unjustifiably been given credit for having delivered a "great" presentation even though my presentation failed to accomplish the objectives defined for the presentation.

IT WAS MAY, 2006, and I was presenting the benefits of a technology solution that my tem and I were trying to sell to one of the world's largest shipping & transportation companies ("The Company"). I did a thorough job of pre-meeting preparation and was convinced that the The Company would see the value in our proposal and award us the business.

By all indications, my delivery of the presentation was flawless: the content was spot-on and compelling, my delivery was smooth and effortless, and there was nary a stutter, "Umm …", or "ya know…" to be heard. In fact, my performance of the presentation was so good that when I finished the presentation, the chief executive in charge of the project said—and I quote: "That was an *excellent* presentation! Your style was so engaging! You had great eye contact, your hand gestures and movements were prefect, you moved about the room in a way that engaged everyone, and your speech and delivery were just great! It was a perfect presentation. I really mean it, you are a great presenter." He continued critiquing and praising my presentation skills for a couple more minutes. Needless to say, I was flattered—even though I found it to be a bit unusual.

After such lavish praise, my team members and I were expecting to hear the executive say that it was such a good presentation that The Company is going to award us the business. So, after thanking him for his feedback and compliments, I said the following: "As we have clearly demonstrated and your team has acknowledged, the [technology] solution will accomplish the objectives for which it is being considered. In addition, the Return on Investment (ROI) exceeds your required threshold and the payback period is 18 months. Let's move forward with the contract process and assemble a team to fully develop the implementation plan."

The executive paused for a moment, looked down at his note pad and said: "Before we do that, can we review the cost-benefit analysis? I'd like to see whether or not this solution meets our ROI threshold." Huh? This was a surprising question because a major portion of the presentation was focused on the solution's cost-benefit analysis and how the solution exceeded The Company's ROI threshold. But somehow, the executive *missed* this major part of the presentation? And if he did, then how could he have given me credit for delivering a "perfect" presentation when—from his perspective—the presentation failed to get him to absorb or understand the cost-benefit data—the main reason he and his team attended the presentation? And if that was the case, then should I have been given credit for having delivered a "great" presentation? I say "No."

From the perspectives of my team and me, this presentation ultimately proved to be bad for me and bad for the audience. It was bad for me because—regardless of how "great" my delivery style—we didn't accomplish our goal to close the deal on-the-spot and I didn't win the business within my necessary timeframe. It was bad for the audience because it delayed the timeframe in which The Company could have started receiving the financial benefits of the solution.

Two Perspectives of a Presentation

The goodness of a presentation can be viewed from two perspectives: (1) the perspective of the **audience** and (2) the perspective of the **presenter**. One could argue that there is a third perspective, namely, that of the entity hiring or scheduling the presenter to speak. However, since the hiring / scheduling entity's purpose for the presentation typically aligns with that of the audience and/or the presenter, I will focus only on the two aforementioned perspectives.

The Audience Perspective

The audience to a presentation most often makes their thoughts on the goodness of a presentation known in the post-presentation feedback surveys they are often asked to complete. These feedback surveys are not a perfect indicator of how "good" or "effective" a presentation or presenter was; oftentimes, audience members are asked to complete these surveys at the end of an event as they are (hurriedly) heading out the door. As a result, the surveys are often hastily completed without providing the degree of thought and diligence that would make the feedback most valuable.

Over the years, I have worked with many companies on the design and distribution of post-presentation audience feedback surveys and, when compiling the audience members' feedback, this is what I commonly find:

- More than half of the surveys are completed hastily with little thought behind the feedback.

- On about half of the surveys, the respondents provide neutral-to-good feedback scores because they don't want to say anything negative about the presenter—even in cases where the respondents believed the presentation and the presenter to be subpar and ineffective.

- Approximately 10% of survey respondents score a presentation and/or presenter harshly based on factors other than the goodness or effectiveness of the presentation or presenter. For example, it is common for respondents to give a generally-agreed "good" presentation and/or presenter a poor rating and write comments such as: "The presenter appeared to be arrogant," or "Her shoes did not match her suit, and it bothered me."

- Approximately 10% of survey respondents provide overly-inflated and undeserved feedback on presentations because they "like" a presenter or feel sorry for a presenter who delivered an embarrassingly awful, ineffective presentation.

- Approximately 20% of survey respondents provide thoughtful, reflective, honest feedback on a presentation or the presenter.

In the end, when feedback surveys are completed in this manner, we end up with semi-meaningless user-feedback surveys that are of limited value as an indicator of the true goodness or effectiveness of a presentation or a presenter.

The best way that I have found to gauge the goodness or effectiveness of a presentation from the audience's perspective is to: (1) clearly identify what it is the audience hopes, expects, and needs to gain from the presentation; and (2) evaluate the presentation based on how effective it was at giving the audience what it hoped, expected, and needed to get from the presentation.

A reliable approach for gauging this degree of effectiveness is to engage the audience in a rigorous post-presentation discussion in an effort to learn whether or not the presenter was able to get the desired message across to the audience, whether or not the audience members gained a clear understanding of the things they needed to understand from the presentation, and whether or not the audience members' purpose for attending the presentation was met.

In my example of the presentation I delivered to The Company, if the evaluation of my presentation's goodness or effectiveness was determined based on how well the audience (in this case, the executive) absorbed and understood the relevant content of the presentation (the cost-benefit and ROI data), then—from the audience / executive's perspective—my presentation should not have been considered to be "effective," and definitely not "perfect." However, if the audience regarded my presentation as being "good" based on how captivating I was as a presenter, then—on some level—my delivery could contribute to the overall goodness- or effectiveness-rating of the presentation.

The Presenter Perspective

When planning and developing a presentation, the presenter will establish goals and/or objectives for the presentation based on the presenter's desired outcome(s) of the presentation. In such cases, the "effectiveness" of a presentation from the presenter perspective is determined based on the presenter's ability to accomplish the pre-presentation-defined desired outcomes of the presentation.

The best approach that I have found for determining the overall "effectiveness" of a presentation from the presenter perspective is to:

(A) Establish the clearly-defined goals, objectives, and desired outcomes of the presentation; these outcomes are defined during the pre-presentation planning process.

(B) Gauge the achievement of the desired outcome(s) of the presentation; this is determined through the post-presentation review process.

By following this approach, the determination of the goodness or effectiveness of a presentation can be achieved by asking one simple question: *Did the presenter accomplish the pre-defined goals, objectives, or desired outcome(s) that were established for the presentation?* If the answer is "Yes," then the presentation can—at a minimum—be considered "effective," regardless of the presenter's delivery style. And if the answer is "No," then—regardless of how polished the presenter's delivery—the presentation should be considered "ineffective."

Think of it this way: Assume that you are a fruits & vegetables sales representative who must sell 10,000 oranges at an upcoming produce trade show in order to keep your job. While preparing for the presentation that you will deliver to a group of produce vendors at the trade show, you define an objective to sell 10,000 oranges to the assembled audience of vendors within one-hour after the presentation's end.

You smoothly-deliver your presentation and everyone in the audience completes feedback surveys that say your presentation delivery style was flawless. Yet, after the presentation when the room clears, you have sold only 200 oranges with no promises from vendors of additional purchases from you. In this case, would you consider your presentation to have been a "good" or "effective" presentation? Even though your presentation delivery style was considered to be good, you will have failed to accomplish your pre-defined desired outcome of the presentation (to sell 10,000 oranges) and, as a result, lost your job.

In this scenario, regardless of how good your presentation *style* was, it didn't matter because you failed to sell the 10,000 oranges and keep your job. I will argue that the achievement of the desired outcome of the presentation was *the most important aspect of the presentation*—from the presenter perspective. The presenter's polished delivery style was an afterthought.

The point to be made from this example is that **the best presentations are those which achieve well-defined goals, objectives, and/or desired outcomes**, and not simply those that look or sound good.

Linking the two Perspectives

Presentation utopia is the state where both the audience's and presenter's goals, objectives, and/or desired outcomes of the presentation are aligned and achieved through the presentation. In this sense, the audience members and the presenter could be considered part of the same community.

A *community* is a group of people who are connected based on common goals, purpose, or interest. And when the presenter-audience community engages in discourse (a formal conversation, discussion, or presentation of mutually-relevant ideas) they become part of a *discourse community*.

As a discourse community, the audience to a presentation and its presenter should be aligned in their interests and desired outcomes of the presentation. When this occurs, it can be said that the *audience perspective* of the presentation and the *presenter perspective* of the presentation are linked, increasing the likelihood that a presentation between this discourse community results in an outcome that is good for both the audience *and* the presenter.

ALIGNMENT BETWEEN PERSPECTIVES

AUDIENCE	PRESENTER
PURPOSE FOR ATTENDING	PURPOSE FOR PRESENTING
DESIRED OUTCOME	DESIRED OUTCOME
SUCCESS CRITERIA	SUCCESS CRITERIA

ALIGNMENT

CH 4

Presentation Pitfalls

Now that we have gained an appreciation for those things that make for a "good" or "effective" presentation, I will shift the focus to review those things that can negatively impact a presentation. Some of the things I review will likely be contradictory to recommendations of things that you may have been taught for many years that are good to do in a presentation. For any such discrepancies, I will make the case for why I believe the detractors I review in this chapter are better excluded from a presentation than included.

Things That Can Hurt or Detract From a Presentation

Since 1985 when I first began to seriously study the art of the presentation, I have seen patterns emerge in the way presentations are delivered and how the incorporation of certain "things" into one's presentation have either consistently helped or hurt a presentation. In this chapter, I will discuss those things that can hurt a presentation—presentation pitfalls.

Understanding pitfalls is important because one cannot develop the most effective presentation possible until he or she understands the things that can detract from a presentation and consciously develops his or her presentation taking these pitfalls into consideration. I once sat through a series of six corporate presentations in one day (yes, it was a very long day), and it seemed as though every presenter, save one, was schooled in the same approach for delivering their talk: (1) they opened with some lame joke that people only laughed at out of politeness or deference to the presenter's job title; (2) they all stated how "excited" they were to be there (it all sounded perfunctory); (3) they all threw in a little profanity in order to relate to the audience; and (4) none of them sounded as though they believed all of the rosy news they shared about the company's near-term and future outlook.

After the presentations, I polled a significant population of the audience members—in confidence—about their honest assessment of the presentations. 90% of the feedback was negative, and the patterns that emerged of things that contributed to overall poor feedback was consistent with the items I described above: the jokes fell flat;

no one believed the presenters were really "excited" to be there (they considered the line to be funny by the time the fourth presenter stated it); the profanity was offensive and inappropriate; and everyone knew the company's outlook was not rosy, so the presenters' credibility was shot. The one presenter whose presentation approach diverged from the other five, however, was given high marks for his honesty and believability.

My study and documentation of presentation pitfalls of the type referenced above have allowed me to provide you with this list of presentation pitfalls that add little-to-no value to a presentation, but contribute significantly to a presentation's ineffectiveness:

Presentation Pitfalls: The List

- Telling jokes
- Laughing at your own humor (especially when no one else does)
- Profanity and sexual comments
- Lack of an understanding of your own content
- Perfunctory comments, towing the company line, and blatant dishonesty
- Inappropriate attire
- Unearned familiarity
- Forgetting your lines or your place in the presentation
- Distracting mannerisms
- Ignoring and not engaging parts of the audience
- Giving handouts during the talk
- Attention-grabbing slides

- Lack of sensitivity to the receiver
- Lack of basic communication skills
- Information overload

Presentation Pitfalls: The Notes

Telling jokes. Somewhere and for some reason, someone told some presenter that telling jokes during a presentation—especially up front as an icebreaker—is a good idea. Telling funny jokes is more than simply writing a joke, delivering it to an audience, and waiting for the uproarious laughter. So the odds of a presenter actually being funny while telling a joke are slim, and the risk of having a joke fall flat far exceeds any benefit one would get from telling a funny joke.

According to stand-up comedy educator and trainer Steve Roye: "There are many truly funny people who find out the hard way that their paper written "jokes" don't work and won't ever work. ... Most people are also under the impression that words and sentences (jokes) can be crafted from a piece a paper and if done properly, then somehow audiences will wet their pants with laughter. Unfortunately, this arcane approach [doesn't work]."

When it comes to telling jokes during a presentation, presenters should ask themselves: Why do I need to tell a joke? What benefit will I get from the joke if people laugh? What harm can I do if the joke falls flat or is ill-received? Is it worth it? What else can I do to get the benefit(s) that I want to get from telling a joke?

Laughing at your own humor (especially when no one else does). In my opinion, the risk of laughing at your own jokes (assuming you are irrational enough to tell a joke in the first place) is that the audience doesn't see the humor in your jokes and they bomb. And when a presenter is the only person laughing at an unsuccessful joke, the presenter looks foolish and loses some credibility—and *credibility* is one of the most important attributes of a presenter.

Lost credibility can negatively impact the overall goodness of a presentation.

Profanity and sexual comments. Using profanity and making sexual comments in front of any audience of more than three of your closest friends is *guaranteed* to offend someone. Why would you, as a presenter, want to knowingly offend your audience members?

A colleague of mine says that we use profanity because we don't know how to otherwise intelligently express ourselves; I believe there is some truth to that statement. By using profanity and making sexual comments the presenter runs the risk of offending the audience, being perceived as somewhat unintelligent & crude, and losing credibility—neither of which is good for a presenter.

Lack of an understanding of your own content. One thing that can damage a presenter's credibility and negatively impact a presentation is a presenter who does not understand the subject matter or content that he or she is presenting. When an audience gets the notion that the presenter is unfamiliar with his or her content, the presenter's perceived and demonstrated credibility is reduced and so too is the audience's perception of the quality of the presenter and the presentation.

Remember: If you show something on a slide, if you

make a statement, or if you share information during your presentation, YOU OWN IT! It becomes *your* material and, therefore, the audience expects that you will be a subject matter expert on *your* content. When you fail to demonstrate an understanding of the content *you* present or show, the audience can feel disappointed that someone has hired an "understudy" to deliver the presentation. When this happens, the presenter loses and, in turn, the audience loses.

Perfunctory statements, towing the company line, and blatant dishonesty. Audiences know when a presenter is spewing disingenuous, throw-away statements that the presenter doesn't really mean but is, instead, making the statements mechanically or robot-like. This can hurt a presenter's perceived honesty and credibility. Why do presenters do this? Because ... well ... the presenter believes that he or she is *supposed* to make such statements.

Think about it: How many times have you heard a presenter use one of the following insincere, perfunctory statements during a presentation? "I'm so excited to be here today." "This is very exciting." (For some reason, presenters like using the words "excited" and "exciting"). "You are the best [your profession] team in the world." "Our products are unmatched in the industry." "No one can compete with us." And, one of my favorites: "You have been a great audience."

Inappropriate attire. As I always say to presenters on the topic of dress and attire: The audience should focus on and remember your *content* not your *costume*!

Men: No zoot suits!!! Not even if you are giving a presentation at a pimp convention. It is *never* okay to wear a zoot suit during a presentation. Wearing such will distract an audience as they will focus only on your suit and not your message.

Women: Be careful with risqué attire (e.g. blouses that show "too much" cleavage) and the length of your mini skirt. Too short, the men will be distracted and the women will think, "tramp!" Either way, you run the risk of distracting the audience or, even worse (whether right or wrong), giving the audience an excuse to question your professionalism or smarts; my research shows that these outcomes are a reality and happen far too often. This is supported by feedback that professional women have given me of things that all women should be cognizant as they contemplate the event and the attending audience.

Unearned familiarity. A presenter must first be given "permission" by an audience to become familiar or chummy with them. Otherwise, familiar comments can be seen as being patronizing.

I once attended a presentation that took place in the state of Georgia where the Brooklyn-born presenter opened his presentation by saying, "How y'all doin'? I'm so glad to be here in the Peach State. Man! When this presentation is over, I'm gonna head out and find myself some good ol' biscuits 'n' grits!" Needless to say, the presentation went downhill from there.

Presenters should first demonstrate to the audience and establish that that aspect of your being is genuine, confirm that the audience buys into it and thus grants you "permission" to become familiar with them. Otherwise, doing so can be a huge turn off to an audience and they could shut down before you even get into your presentation.

Forgetting your lines or your place in the presentation. Although losing one's place during a presentation or forgetting your lines is forgivable, such moments are awkward for both the audience and the presenter. These moments can lead an audience to believe that the presenter does not have a mastery of her or his content and, therefore, is not as credible on the subject matter; this can hurt the presentation.

Distracting mannerisms. Using hand gestures, facial expressions, vocal inflection, and other presentation enhancements can have a positive impact on the audience's reception of your presentation and your message. However, wild hand gestures, pointless hand gestures, flailing arms, nervous twitches, misinterpreted facial expressions, nervous laughter, and other untrained mannerisms can become a distraction during a presentation. Hand gestures, facial expressions, vocal inflection, and other mannerisms should be executed with purpose and related to the content being delivered.

Ignoring or not engaging parts of the audience. During the presentation, the presenter must constantly be aware of the degree to which he or she is engaging the audience. This can be as simple as sharing eye contact with audience members in all parts of the room, and—depending on the size and configuration of the room—walking to the right, left, middle, front and back of the room as appropriate and possible.

Audience feedback from post-presentation surveys

and interviews I have conducted over the years suggest that audience members can feel "slighted," "devalued," and "disrespected" when a presenter presents with his or her back to the audience members or never makes the audience members feel as though they are an important part of the experience. When this happens, audience members can form unfavorable impressions of the presenter and presentation.

Giving handouts during the talk. Although not always a bad thing, handing out documents or other collateral during a presentation can do more harm than good. The natural instinct for audience members when they receive such collateral is to read and peruse it; this takes their attention away from the presenter and the message being communicated. The result is oftentimes an audience that is not fully informed because they may have been distracted (by the handouts) from the delivery of the presenter's message.

Attention-grabbing slides. In Chapter 13: *Presentation Slides: Best Practices,* I provide greater detail on the subject of presentation slides. In my opinion, presentation slides should mostly be used as a guide for the presentation—a vehicle for helping the audience (and the presenter) follow the presentation message as it is being delivered by the presenter. The biggest mistake presenters make when it comes to the use of PowerPoint or other slides is making the slides too attention-grabbing. One might think that this is a good thing—having attention-grabbing slides—and sometimes it is. But mostly, it is not.

Take a look at the following two slides.

A

WHAT WE DO

B

WHAT WE DO

+ SALES
+ TRAINING
+ STRATEGY
+ CONSULTING

What happened when you looked at the two slides? If you are like other people, you spent much more time *staring* at slide A than you did *looking* at slide B. This is a natural reaction from audience members when they are presented with detailed attention-grabbing slides such as slide A. Sure, it's fancier, prettier, and more attention-grabbing than slide B, but considering that both slides are intended to convey the same information—the services this presenter's company offers—slide B does so more easily, cleanly, simplistically, and effectively than the fancy attention-grabbing slide A. Slide B is also less distracting than slide A. When people ask why I rarely use complex, overly-fancy, attention grabbing slides during my presentations, I tell them it is because I want the audience to pay attention to *me* and the message I am trying to convey, and not be distracted by my slides.

Lack of sensitivity to the receiver. I once attended a presentation that was delivered by a man who said during the presentation, "… so some of you Oriental girls in the audience might appreciate that." *Oriental girls*??!! I was surprised that such a seasoned presenter would make such an insensitive and ignorant comment during a presentation in which there were professional Asian *women* (not "girls") in the audience. It should go without saying that those Asian women in the audience instantly disregarded and tuned-out the insensitive presenter.

Lack of basic communication skills. I am a firm believer that a presentation's content is king. However, effective communication skills and presentation style can positively (or negatively) influence an audience's receptivity to and perception of a presentation.

By *basic communication skills* I am referring to the ability to articulate thoughts, ideas, and feelings, as well as the ability to listen. A presenter who mumbles, for example, may not be as effective at communicating his or her message as someone who articulates effectively. A presenter who prattles may cause an audience to lose interest and will not be as effective as a presenter who self-edits and is brief. A presenter who over-talks an audience member's question or comment can be seen as insensitive or rude. A presenter who neglects eye contact with the audience could be perceived as being disengaged and disinterested.

Information overload. An audience has a limited capacity to absorb and retain an amount of information in a given amount of time. I call this the *audience information capacity per hour*.

As I have observed, audience members can most effectively absorb and retain the content of one PowerPoint slide (or its equivalent in a visual aid or an information dissemination vehicle) within a 3-minute window. In other words, presenters should only use one slide for every 3 minute interval of the presentation's total duration.

For example, a presenter who attempts to explain the details of *Homer's Iliad and Odyssey* in a 15-minute presentation would fail because of the amount of information the presenter would have to provide the audience within a 15-minute window. And when an audience is presented with more information than they can effectively absorb in a given window of time, the audience gets mentally fatigued and much of the information gets lost and wasted in the process.

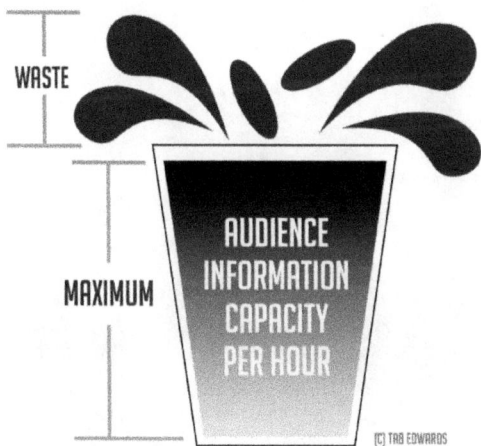

INFORMATION OVERLOAD?

WASTE

MAXIMUM

AUDIENCE
INFORMATION
CAPACITY
PER HOUR

(C) TAB EDWARDS

PART TWO

The Presentation Conjunction™

CH 5

The Presentation Conjunction™

The *Presentation Conjunction™* is the model I developed for describing and illustrating the association, conjunction, and interrelationship between the major constituents of a presentation. Each constituent (listed below) holds an influential relationship with another, thereby creating a co-dependent system that leads to the development and delivery of an effective presentation.

The major constituents of a presentation include:

- Purpose, Goal, Objective(s)
- Desired Outcome
- Presentation Type
- Presentation Elements
- Experience and Learning

Purpose, Goal, Objective

Purpose: The presentation purpose—from both the audience and presenter perspectives—gives direction to the presentation, guides expectations of both its presenter and the audience, and helps ensure that the presentation is being developed and delivered toward the mutual goals of the audience and presenter. The presentation purpose answers the questions: Why is this presentation being delivered? Why does the presentation matter to the audience and the presenter?

Goal: The presentation goal is the specific, intended result of the presentation. It is the general statement of a broad intended outcome, and it takes the form of an action verb (e.g. The goal of this presentation is *to increase the sale* of programmable thermostats by educating the audience on their importance in reducing home utility costs).

Objective: The presentation objective is intended to support the presentation goal and/or purpose. Objectives should be "S.M.A.R.T."—Specific, Measurable, Attainable, Realistic, and Time bound. For example, an objective that is defined to support the presentation goal stated in the example above could read: The objective of this presentation is to persuade the audience members to purchase $50,000 in programmable thermostats within 2-hours after the end of the presentation.

A presentation's purpose, goal, and objectives should align with and support the audience's and presenter's *desired outcome* of the presentation.

Desired Outcome

The desired outcome of a presentation is the "This is what I want to happen" event from the perspective of both the audience and presenter. It can be articulated by asking and answering the following question depending on your perspective:

- Audience Perspective: "When I leave this presentation I want to [fill in the blank]."

- Presenter Perspective: "When this presentation is over, I want [fill in the blank]."

The desired outcome of a presentation should align with and influence the *type of presentation* that is delivered.

Presentation Type

As written in Chapter 1: *Speech vs. Presentation*, the purpose of a presentation dictates its type, and there are four primary purposes of a presentation:

- **To Inform.** To make the audience aware of something; to communicate information with the intent to educate the audience; to share information that the audience will find to be interesting and of value. A presentation with the purpose is to inform is called an *Informative* or *Educational Presentation*.

- **To Motivate.** To energize, inspire, or move the audience to take an action; to increase the audience's interest in engaging or reengaging in something; to entertain the audience. A presentation with the purpose to motivate is called a *Motivational Presentation*.

- **To Persuade.** To urge the audience to follow a certain or desired course of action; to convince the audience that a certain course of action is favorable to another; to influence the audience's way of thinking about or believing something. A presentation with the purpose to persuade is called a *Persuasive Presentation.*

- **To Demonstrate.** To provide the audience with an understanding of how something works; to show the audience how to perform an act or use something. A presentation with the purpose to demonstrate is called a *Demonstrative* or *Instructional Presentation.*

Presentation Elements

As I wrote previously, the most important aspect of a presentation is the presentation's ability to achieve the well-defined goals, objectives, and/or desired outcomes that the presentation is designed to achieve from both the presenter's and the audience's perspectives. In my experience, the most important elements of a presentation—related to the successful achievement of the presentation's goals, objectives, and desired outcomes—are the (in order of importance):

1. Content and its Design
2. Message Delivery
3. Speaker Credibility
4. Presenter Style
5. Audience Engagement

Content and Design

As I hope to demonstrate throughout this book, *Content is King!* In the context of a presentation, *content* is the subject matter and the topics to be covered in a presentation. People attend most presentations based on the content that is expected to be delivered through the presentation. And if the primary reason why people attend presentations is the message or information they expect to receive (messaging and information that make up the content), it stands to reason that the most important element of a presentation is its content.

The manner in which a presentation's content is designed (phrased, arranged, illustrated, delivery-ordered, related to the purpose) contributes to the presenter's and, ultimately, the presentation's overall effectiveness at ensuring the audience absorbs and comprehends its content.

Message Delivery

Message delivery is about ensuring that the message in your presentation's content and your approach for sharing the content satisfy the audience's desired outcome of the presentation as well as your desired outcome of the presentation. It's about providing a level of understanding and, most importantly, it's about relevance to the audience and relevance to the achievement of the presentation goals and objectives.

Speaker Credibility

Although the credibility of the presenter could be considered as a sub-element of either Message Delivery or Audience Engagement, I am calling it out separately because of the impact a presenter's credibility can have on the audience's ultimate absorption of the presentation message and content.

Credibility is the quality of being believable and/or trustworthy. It is also the believability of the statements made by the presenter as well as their actions. A "credible" presenter is considered expert (experienced, qualified, intelligent and skilled) and trustworthy (honest, fair and caring). And being a credible source of information can significantly influence the actions on the part of audience members. In addition, a presenter's credibility influences the audience's perception of the effectiveness or goodness of the presenter's presentation which automatically gives the presenter higher ratings than those given for a non-"expert" who has given the exact same presentation.

Presenter Style

Style is the vehicle available to the presenter that he or she can use to connect with the audience. It is the shell in which the presentation is delivered. It is the presenter's delivery skill; it is the presenter's demeanor; it is the presenter's attire; it is the presenter's articulation; it is the presenter's demonstrated knowledge of the content and subject matter; it is the way the presenter eases you into the discussion.

True, these things play second-fiddle to the presentation's content, but they wrap the content in a cloak that enhances the goodness of the content. I liken style to a great meal: the presentation of a gourmet meal somehow contributes to our overall impression of the goodness of the meal. Just as "we eat first with our eyes," so too do "we enhance our listening with our eyes."

Audience Engagement

The most effective presentations are those where the audience is actively engaged and personally invested in the presentation. The challenge for the presenter is to figure out how to accomplish this.

Experience and Learning

The repeated process of: defining the presentation purpose, goals, and objectives; using these definitions to determine the desired outcomes of the presentation; using the desired outcome of the presentation to settle on the appropriate presentation type; and defining, embodying, and executing the elements of the presentation all contribute to the experience and learning that take place by the presenter. And it is this experience and learning that contribute to the presenter's growth and development as a presenter and speaker.

This growth and development will ultimately help the presenter become better at defining goals & objectives, establishing productive desired outcomes, executing the presentation elements, and delivering continually-improving presentations. This is the *Presentation Conjunction*.

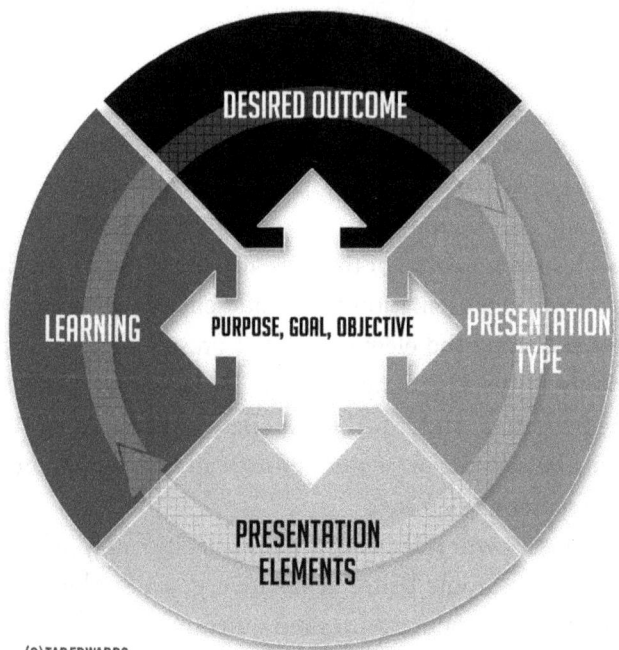

PRESENTATION ECOSYSTEM

DESIRED OUTCOME

LEARNING   PURPOSE, GOAL, OBJECTIVE   PRESENTATION TYPE

PRESENTATION ELEMENTS

(C)TABEDWARDS

PART THREE

Considerations for Developing an Effective Presentation

CH 6

The Parts of a Presentation

A well-considered presentation is made up of more parts than simply the introduction, the body, and the close. A presentation includes activities involved in the preparation, the creation, the call to action, and validation that the goals and objectives of the presentation have been accomplished; this is in addition to the presentation introduction, body, and the close.

The Parts of a Presentation

Pre-Session

1. Preparation
2. Development

In-Session

3. Introduction
4. Body
5. Call to Action
6. Close

Post-Session

7. Validate the accomplishment of goals & objectives or develop a plan to do so.

Each of these stages and elements of a presentation holds a supporting relationship with another:

- The *Pre-Session Preparation* supports the Presentation Development process and the overall presentation activity.

- The *Presentation Development* process supports the In-session Content of the presentation (the introduction, body, call to action, and close) as well as the purpose, goals, objectives, and desired outcomes of the presentation.

- The *In-session presentation activities* (the content delivery and Question & Answer session) support and influence the desired outcomes of the presentation (e.g. the goals and objectives)

- The *Post-session Validation* (that the purpose, goals, objectives, and desired outcomes of the presentation have been achieved) help determine whether or not the presentation was "successful"—with success being defined as the achievement of the predefined purpose, goals, objectives, and desired outcome of a presentation from the audience and presenter perspectives.

PARTS OF A PRESENTATION

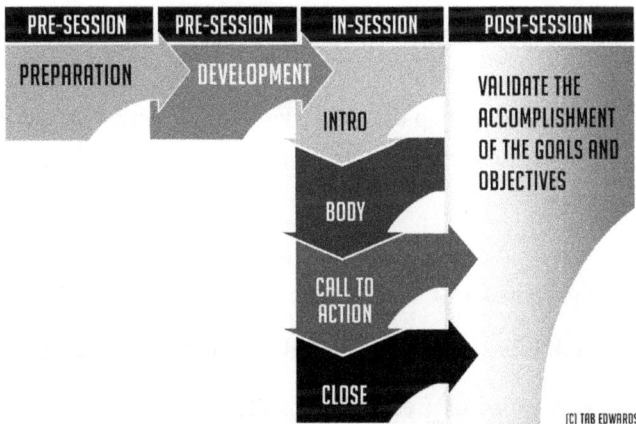

PRE-SESSION	PRE-SESSION	IN-SESSION	POST-SESSION
PREPARATION	DEVELOPMENT	INTRO	VALIDATE THE ACCOMPLISHMENT OF THE GOALS AND OBJECTIVES
		BODY	
		CALL TO ACTION	
		CLOSE	

(C) TAB EDWARDS

Pre-Session: Preparation

Pre-session Preparation is the process of planning for the development of the presentation content and the actual in-session presentation delivery. Pre-session Preparation involves asking and answering the following questions of your presentation:

- What is the purpose of this presentation—from the audience and presenter perspectives?

- What are the goals, objectives, and desired outcomes of this presentation– from the audience and presenter perspectives?

- What audience questions and/or objections should I prepare for?

- Will I need to provide handouts or other collateral?

- What type of presentation will I deliver?

- What will I do if my presentation time is suddenly cut in half?

- How big is the expected audience? This will impact the audio-visual needs of the presentation (e.g. hand-held microphone, clip-on microphone, no microphone, slides, flipchart, whiteboard), the communication tools used, the visual aids needed, the physical layout of the venue (which can influence your delivery approach), and time allocated to questions and answers.

- What is the physical layout of the venue? Can I influence the layout? Some physical layout arrangements (e.g. classroom style, conference room style, auditorium style) can either facilitate or limit your interaction and engagement with the audience.

- If my communication vehicle (e.g. the PC or projector used to project your slides) is inoperable or dies mid-session, what is my back-up plan?

- Should I plant a "ringer" in the audience to ask me an important question or to offer a testimonial related to the topic of my presentation?

- What should I wear?

- How much time should I allocate for practice?

These are the questions I ask myself prior to a presentation. Anything that you can think of that will help you prepare, prepare for, and/or deliver your presentation should be addressed as you prepare for your session.

Pre-Session: Development

In Part Four of this book, I discuss the *Presentation Development Process* in greater detail. For now, I will share that the process of developing the in-session presentation activity (which is more than just the delivery of the presentation content) includes the following stages:

1. Define the presentation purpose, goals, and objectives

2. Define the desired outcome(s) of the presentation

3. Define the type of presentation to deliver

4. Develop the presentation content

5. Create your presentation outline and/or sample slides

6. Validate that the content of your presentation aligns with the purpose, goals, objectives, and desired outcomes

7. Prepare for the delivery of the presentation

8. Ensure that your message is being absorbed by the audience

9. Determine how you will connect with the audience

This process is illustrated in the diagram below.

Presentation Development Process

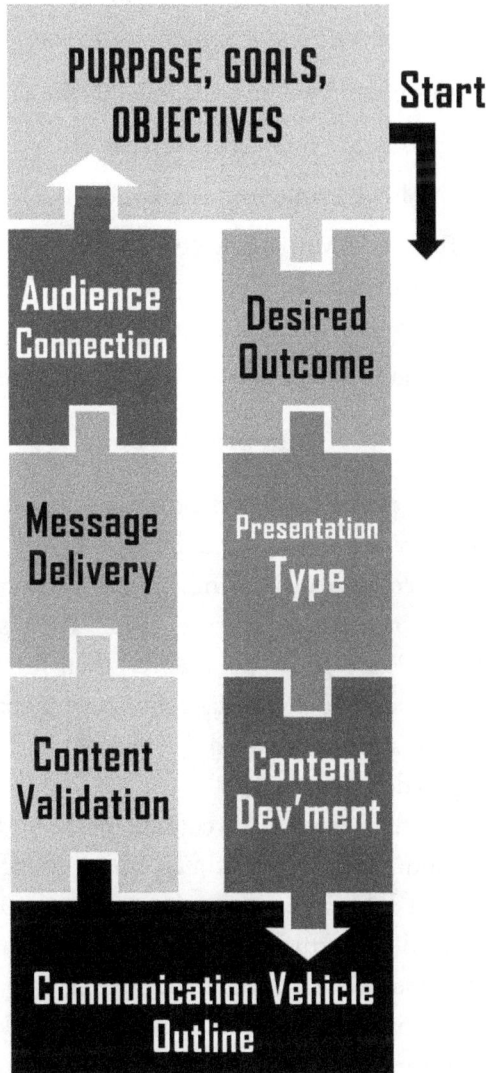

PURPOSE, GOALS, OBJECTIVES

Start

Audience Connection

Desired Outcome

Message Delivery

Presentation Type

Content Validation

Content Dev'ment

Communication Vehicle Outline

In-Session: Introduction

The presentation *Introduction* is where the presenter sets the stage for what the audience is about to experience. The introduction should tell the audience:

- This is why you are attending this presentation
- This is what you will experience today
- This is why you should care about this session
- This is why you should give my message credence (establishing credibility)
- Watch as I surreptitiously lead you from this introduction into the content of my presentation

In-Session: Body

The *Body* of a presentation is the meat of the presentation. It is where the message and the influence of the presentation are contained. The "influence" of the presentation is dictated by the type of presentation. For instance, if the presentation type is "persuasive," then the body of the presentation should contain the content that will influence the audience toward the thought and/or behavior that you desire.

When developing the content for the body of the presentation, remember that *facts trump opinion,* so whenever you have an opportunity to back your assertions with credible factual data, I recommend that you do so. And if you do elect to offer your (professional or expert) opinion of something—if it cannot be backed by credible research or factual data—then state your experience that gives you right to offer an opinion that the audience should consider believable or credible. And always re-member my number one rule for presentation content: **Know of what you speak and show, or don't.** In other words, the presenter should understand and be able to justify and explain *everything* that he or she speaks of or shows on a slide. And if the presenter cannot, then he or she should either get answers about the content, remove the content from the presentation, or refrain from speak-ing about something that he or she does not understand or cannot answer questions about.

Remember: **If you show it, you own it**.

In-Session: Call to Action

The *Call-to-Action* is where the presenter asks something specific of the audience. Does the presenter want the au-dience to purchase something? Does the presenter want the audience to sign-up for something? Does the pre-senter want the audience to engage with him or her on something? Does the presenter want the audience to visit a website? The action that the presenter wants the audi-ence to take after participating in the presentation should be clearly defined and justified.

The Call-to-Action answers the following questions:

- What is the action that I want the audience to take after participating in this presentation?

- Did I explicitly make that point or provide instruc-tion during the presentation?

- Did the presentation unambiguously state the action

I want the audience to engage in?

- Did the presentation make the case for why the audience should engage in the behavior that I defined?

In-Session: The Close

The presentation *Close* is best described as the ribbon that is wrapped around a present; if the presentation was effectively delivered, then the wrap-up should be a formality.

The *close* is where the presenter asks him or herself:

- Did I cover everything that I intended?

- How effective was I at delivering on the goals and objectives of the presentation?

- How do I know whether or not I have been effective?

- Does the audience have a clear understanding of what is expected of them?

- How confident am I that the audience will act in the manner which I hope? Do I need to revisit this part of my presentation?

- Am I prepared for the questions I am likely to receive in the Q&A session?

- Are there any loose ends that I need to tie before ending this presentation?

Post-Session: Validate the Accomplishment of the Goals & Objectives

Post-session *Validation* is the process of determining any of the following:

- Did I accomplish the goals and objectives of the presentation from the audience perspective?

- Did I accomplish the goals and objectives of the presentation that I defined for myself and my team?

- How will I know whether or not I accomplished the goals and objectives of the presentation (from both perspectives)?

- If I did not accomplish the goals and objectives of the presentation (from either perspective), then what is my plan of action to do so post-presentation?

- If I did not accomplish the goals and objectives of the presentation (from either perspective), then why was I unsuccessful? How do I adjust for the reason(s) going forward?

PART FOUR

The Presentation Development Process

In this section of the book I will provide a proven process and guide for developing effective presentations

CH 7

Stage 1
Define the Purpose, Goals, Objectives, and Desired Outcome

For this part of the book, **I strongly recommend** that you document your answers to the questions contained herein. Using a tool such as Microsoft Word, OpenOffice Writer (a free tool that is similar to and compatible with MS Word), or pen & paper will make the content and presentation development process easier.

I also recommend the use of the **SNaP Presenter** presentation tool to facilitate and streamline the presentation development process. *SNaP Presenter* is a PC-based software application that is the companion to this book. It automates the presentation development process (including the auto-creation of your MS PowerPoint or OpenOffice Impress presentation slides) by asking a series of questions about your presentation. *SNaP Presenter* makes the creation (and ultimate delivery) of your presentation extremely easy, while at the same time helping you to become a better presenter in the process.

Purpose, Goals, Objectives

Purpose

The presentation *purpose*—from both the audience and presenter perspectives—gives direction to the presentation, guides expectations of both its presenter and the audience, and helps ensure that the presentation is being developed and delivered toward the mutual goals of the audience and presenter.

Answer the following questions to define the presentation purpose:

1. Why is this presentation being delivered?

2. Why does the presentation matter to the audience and the presenter?

To articulate the purpose of the presentation, use your answers to the questions above as input to complete the following sentence; this applies to both the audience and presenter perspectives:

3. The purpose of this presentation is to [complete the sentence]

Goal

The presentation goal is the specific, intended result of the presentation. It is the general statement of a broad intended outcome, and it takes the form of an action verb (e.g. *The goal of this presentation is to increase the sale of programmable thermostats by educating the audience on their importance in reducing home utility costs*).

To define the *goal* of the presentation, answer the following questions:

1. **What do I need to accomplish through this presentation? [Presenter perspective]**

2. **What does the audience need to gain from this presentation? [Audience perspective]**

3. **Why do I <u>need</u> to give this presentation? [Presenter perspective]**

4. **Why does the audience <u>need</u> to participate in this presentation? [Audience perspective]**

To articulate the goal of the presentation, use your answers to the questions above as input to complete the following sentence; this applies to both the audience and presenter perspectives:

5. **The goal of this presentation is to [complete the sentence]**

Objective

The presentation objective is intended to support the presentation goal and/or purpose. Objectives should be "S.M.A.R.T."—Specific, Measurable, Attainable, Realistic, and Time bound. For example, an objective that is defined to support the presentation goal stated in the example above could read: *The objective of this presentation* *is to persuade the audience members to purchase $50,000 in programmable thermostats within 2-hours after the end of the presentation.*

To define the objective(s) of the presentation, use the goal you defined above as a guide and answer the following questions:

1. **What quantifiable, S.M.A.R.T. results—related to the goal—do I want to achieve based on this presentation? [Presenter perspective]**

2. **What quantifiable, S.M.A.R.T. results—related to the goal—do I want to learn how to achieve based on this presentation? [Audience perspective; optional]**

To articulate the objective(s) of the presentation, use your answers to the questions above as input to complete the following sentence; this applies to both the audience and presenter perspectives:

3. **The objective of this presentation is to [complete the sentence using the S.M.A.R.T. model]**

A presentation's purpose, goal, and objectives should align with and support the audience's and presenter's *desired outcome* of the presentation.

Desired Outcome

The desired outcome of a presentation is the "This is what I want to happen" event from the perspective of both the audience and presenter.

To articulate the desired outcome of the presentation, answer the following questions depending on your perspective:

1. **Audience Perspective: "When I leave this presentation I want to [complete the sentence]."**

2. **Presenter Perspective: "When this presentation is over, I want [complete the sentence]."**

The desired outcome of a presentation should align with and influence the *type of presentation* that is delivered.

CH 8

Stage 2
Determine the Presentation Type

After defining the presentation purpose, goals, objectives, and desired outcome, determine the appropriate *Presentation Type* for the presentation. The type of presentation you develop is related to and should satisfy the presentation *purpose*, support the accomplishment of the presentation *goals* & *objectives*, and deliver on the *desired outcome* of the presentation.

Presentation Purpose / Type

- **To Inform.** To make the audience aware of something; to communicate information with the intent to educate the audience; to share information that the audience will find to be interesting and of value. A presentation with the purpose is to inform is called an *Informative or Educational Presentation*.

- **To Motivate.** To energize, inspire, or move the audience to take an action; to increase the audience's interest in engaging or reengaging in something; to entertain the audience. A presentation with the purpose to motivate is called a *Motivational Presentation*.

- **To Persuade.** To urge the audience to follow a certain or desired course of action; to convince the audience that a certain course of action is favorable to another; to influence the audience's way of thinking about or believing something. A presentation with the purpose to persuade is called a *Persuasive Presentation*.

- **To Demonstrate.** To provide the audience with an understanding of how something works; to show the audience how to perform an act or use something. A presentation with the purpose to demonstrate is called a *Demonstrative* or *Instructional Presentation*.

As you develop your presentation, you should continually refer to the presentation type in order to ensure that the presentation you are developing is the type of presentation you intended based on the presentation purpose, goal, objectives, and desired outcome.

CH 9

Stage 3
Content Development

Think? Know? Prove?

The "honesty-checking" activities to which I refer in this section of the book introduce the **Think? Know? Prove?** (T-K-P) concept and are designed to force an added level of diligence and rigor to critical stages in the presentation content development process. The T-K-P process is designed to ensure that the presentation you develop has the highest odds of achieving the goals and objectives of the presentation by forcing the discipline of validating ("honesty-checking") the strength of your content and position in the presentation development process.

What we *Think* (what we believe or suppose), our level of *Knowledge* (familiarity, awareness, or understanding gained through experience or study) and that for which we have *Proof* (the act of validating. Finding or testing the truth of something) can be used as measures of the level of diligence we apply to ensuring that the presentation content is most powerful related to the purpose, goals, objectives, and desired outcomes of the presentation.

What we *Think* to be the case about something is less reliable and, therefore, less useful than what we can *Prove* to be the case about something. So, if we only *Think* that something is valid, it should raise a **red flag** as being something that we need to dig into further in order to validate—as best we can—that something is indeed as claimed.

Definitions of Think, Know, and Prove are provided below:

- **Think.** To suppose or assume "something" based on some *rational logic* or information.

- **Know.** To perceive or understand "something" to be valid based on *experience*.

- **Prove.** To establish the "something" as being valid based on *evidence*.

As an example, let's assume that some research scientist was fed up with listening to his Prius-driving, vegetarian relatives rant about how they only eat vegetables because they could never harm another living creature—including animals—just to satisfy their hunger. So, in order to silence his vegetarian relatives, the scientist developed a hypothesis that he has always believed: *Plants are "living creatures" that feel pain, too, and therefore can be harmed.*

Applying the T-K-P activity against this hypothesis, the research scientist got the following:

Hypothesis: *Plants are living creatures that feel pain*

1. What do I **THINK?** I think that plants feel pain; it seems logical.

2. What do I **KNOW?** We know that plants, including vegetables, feel pain when subjected to trauma such as being yanked out of the ground, peeled, cooked and eaten.

3. What can I **PROVE?** Vegetables and plants initiate a massive hormone and chemical barrage internally when they suffer any kind of injury. This response is akin to the nerve response and endorphin release when an animal is injured. Therefore, concludes the research scientist, vegetarians would starve if they didn't eat any "living creatures."

Applying the Think? Know? Prove? rigor to the presentation content development process will help you determine just how closely-aligned and relevant your planned content is to the purpose, goals, objectives, and desired outcomes of the presentation.

Developing Presentation Content

Using the purpose, goals, objectives, and desired outcomes you defined above for the presentation, answer the questions below to develop relevant, meaningful, power-ful content.

1. Based on the <u>AUDIENCE'S</u> pre-determined pur-pose, goals, and objectives for attending, listening to, or participating in your presentation, complete the sentence: "By attending, listening to, or partici-pating in this presentation, the audience hopes to ___ "

   - List up to three things

2. **Select one of the following statements based on your answers to question #1 above:**

   - I THINK these are the audience's primary rea-sons for attending the presentation. [If this op-tion is selected it is a **red flag**: you need to vali-date the list to improve your position here]

   - I KNOW that these are the audience's primary reasons for attending the presentation.

   - I can PROVE that these are the audience's prima-ry reasons for attending the presentation.

   - Explain and justify your selection [*Best practice*: write the answer down]

3. Based on <u>YOUR</u> pre-determined purpose, goals, and objectives for delivering your presentation, complete the sentence: "After this presentation is over, I want the audience to ___ "

   - List up to three things

4. Using the table below, match the audience's purpose, goals, objectives, and desired outcome of the presentation to your purpose, goals, objectives, and desired outcome for the presentation:

Alignment Checking

Audience Purpose	Your Purpose	Alignment or Match?
		Yes | No

Audience Goal(s)	Your Goal(s)	Alignment or Match?
		Yes | No
		Yes | No
		Yes | No

Audience Objective(s)	Your Objective(s)	Alignment or Match?
		Yes | No
		Yes | No
		Yes | No

Audience Desired Outcome	Your Desired Outcome	Alignment or Match?
		Yes | No
		Yes | No

For each Purpose, Goal, Objective, and Desired Outcome, if you answered "No Alignment / Match" then this is a **red flag** and you should revisit the purpose, goals, and objectives to ensure that those of the audience align with or match yours.

5. **Select one of the following statements based on your alignment /matching in question #4 above:**

    - Yes, my purpose, goals, objectives, and desired outcome align with each of the audience's purpose, goals, objectives, and desired outcome.

    - No, there is at least one of my purpose, goals, objectives, or desired outcome that does not align with / match the audience's [if this option is selected, this is a **red flag**]

    If your selection is "No," rethink your purpose, goals, objectives, and/or desired outcome to bring them into alignment with the audience's, and document your new purpose, goals, objectives, and/or desired outcome.

6. **List up to twelve (12) TOPICS you plan to review or discuss in your presentation**

    A **"topic"** is the subject of conversation that the presenter will discuss with the audience. A **"theme"** is a unifying idea that consists of one or more topics.

    So, for instance, the *theme* of a conversation could be "The need for clean drinking water in society," and the *topics* that support this theme could be "What is 'clean' drinking water?" and "The benefits of clean drinking water."

THEME - TOPIC RELATIONSHIP

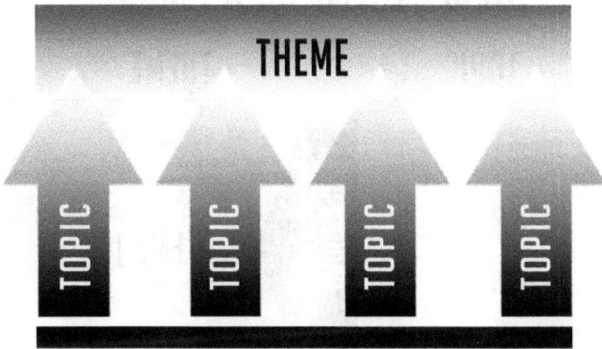

(C) TAB EDWARDS

Why *twelve* (12) topics for this activity? My experience has shown that the most effective presentations are those which are comprised of three to four major THEMES, and the pace of the presentation of each theme flows and is absorbed best by the audience when supported by three to four TOPICS; more than four topics become confusing and are not as easily absorbed by the audience, and fewer than three topics is often not enough to completely convey an idea.

For this part of the process, your twelve topics should cover the entirety of the content or information you plan to review during your presentation.

7. **Group the TOPICS from question #6 into three (3) or four (4) groups or buckets based on common THEMES or ideas. Your groupings should look something like this**

TOPIC - THEME GROUPINGS

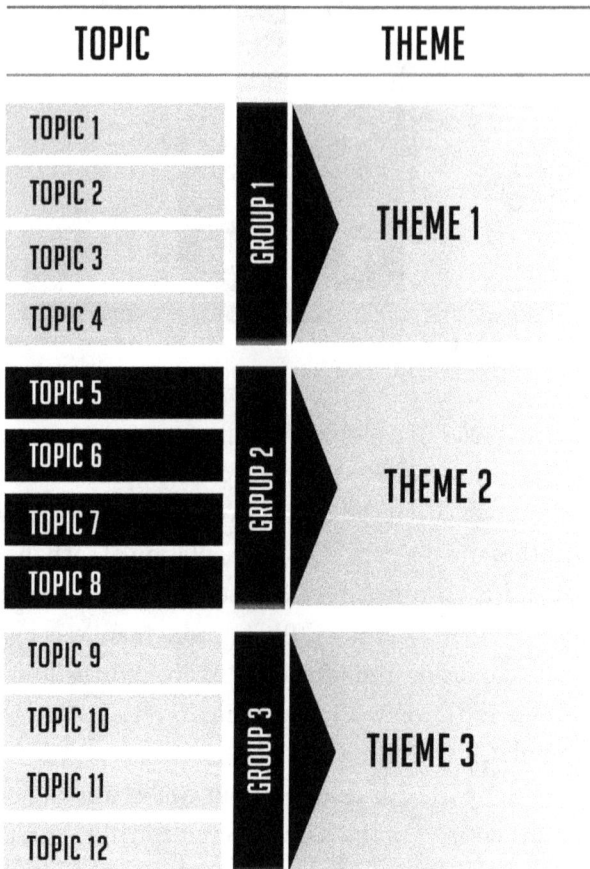

TOPIC	THEME
TOPIC 1	
TOPIC 2	GROUP 1 → THEME 1
TOPIC 3	
TOPIC 4	
TOPIC 5	
TOPIC 6	GRPUP 2 → THEME 2
TOPIC 7	
TOPIC 8	
TOPIC 9	
TOPIC 10	GROUP 3 → THEME 3
TOPIC 11	
TOPIC 12	

(C) TAB EDWARDS

8. Based on your groupings of the TOPICS (Group/ Theme 1, 2, 3, and/or 4) as developed in question #7, define the THEMES of your presentation by giving Group/Theme 1, 2, 3, and 4 THEME NAMES based on that which each Group's/Theme's TOPICS have in common.

For example:

TOPIC - THEME GROUPINGS

TOPIC		THEME NAME
LOBSTER SALMON SEA BASS SHRIMP	GROUP 1	SEAFOOD
CARROTS SPINACH TURNIPS BROCCOLI	GRPUP 2	VEGETABLES
CAKE PIE ICE CREAM FRUIT	GROUP 3	DESSERT

(C) TAB EDWARDS

Name each of your THEMES:

- Group 1 THEME = [Give the Group/Theme a name]

- Group 2 THEME = [Give the Group/Theme a name]

- Group 3 THEME = [Give the Group/Theme a name]

- Group 4 THEME = [Give the Group/Theme a name]

9. **Align your planned discussion TOPICS to the audience purpose, goals, objective(s), and/or desired outcome of the presentation. Do this for both the AUDIENCE and for YOU.**

Ask yourself: Does my TOPIC 1 align with an audience purpose, goal, objective, or desired outcome? If you answer "No" to any, this is a **red flag**.

See the table on the adjacent page for an example.

Topic—Theme Alignment

THEME 1	Does Each TOPIC Align With or Match an <u>Audience </u>Purpose/Goal/Objective / or Desired Outcome?	RESULT
Topic 1	ALIGNS WITH THE PURPOSE	Ok
Topic 2	ALIGNS WITH A GOAL	Ok
Topic 3	ALIGNS WITH A DESIRED OUTCOME	Ok
Topic 4	**NO ALIGNMENT**	Red Flag

THEME 2

Topic 5	ALIGNS WITH AN OBJECTIVE	Ok
Topic 6	**NO ALIGNMENT**	Red Flag
Topic 7	ALIGNS WITH THE PURPOSE	Ok
Topic 8	**NO ALIGNMENT**	Red Flag

THEME 3

Topic 9	ALIGNS WITH A GOAL	Ok
Topic 10	ALIGNS WITH THE DESIRED OUTCOME	Ok
Topic 11	ALIGNS WITH THE DESIRED OUTCOME	Ok
Topic 12	ALIGNS WITH A GOAL	Ok

If there is no alignment or match for a TOPIC, revisit questions #1 through #6 to ensure that you have defined the most relevant planned discussion TOPICS.

10. **For each TOPIC you defined in question #6, provide a description for each. The description should briefly explain what you plan to discuss about each topic.**

For example:

Theme/Topic	Description
Sea Food (Theme)	**Sub-Topics**
Lobster (Topic)	• I will discuss the origins of lobster as a food item • I will discuss the nutritional benefits of eating lobster • I will discuss the various types of lobster we eat most often and their typical prices • I will discuss the major sources of lobster and why they are so expensive.
Salmon (Topic)	Description
Sea Bass (Topic)	Description
Shrimp (Topic)	Description

11. **For each TOPIC, determine whether or not it directly contributes to fulfilling the <u>audience's</u> purpose, goals, objectives, and desired outcomes of the presentation. Does each TOPIC directly contribute to fulfilling <u>your</u> purpose, goals, objectives, and desired outcomes of the presentation, too?**

If the answer for any TOPIC is "No," then this should be a **red flag** item that requires further consideration. Revisit questions #1 through #9 as you do so.

12. **Describe how discussing each TOPIC will help to accomplish the <u>audience's</u> purpose, goals, objectives (as relevant), and desired outcomes of the presentation.**

Developing the Communication Vehicle / Visual Aids Outline

The **Communication Vehicle** is the supporting platform that you will use to guide your presentation. Examples of communication vehicles include: flipcharts, PowerPoint slides, photo projectors, video, audio, handouts, and brochures just to name a few.

For business presentations and most other stand-up presentations, PowerPoint or OpenOffice Impress slides are the most frequently used vehicles. For other presentations (or speeches), simple notes are commonly used by the presenter.

13. **Will you be using presentation slides (such as Microsoft PowerPoint or OpenOffice Impress)?**

If the answer is "No," you can answer questions #15, 16, and 17. However, I recommend that you answer each question in this section.

14. What is the duration of your presentation (in minutes)?

- Divide the duration (in minutes) of your presentation by three (3) to calculate the recommended number of slides to use in your presentation. Experience shows that—on average—a presenter will most effectively complete the discussion of the contents of one slide in three minutes. For example, if your presentation's duration is 60 minutes, then the recommended number of content slides you should use for your presentation should not exceed twenty (20).

HOW MANY SLIDES TO USE?

PRESENTATION DURATION (IN MINUTES)		RECOMMENDED MINUTES PER SLIDE		RECOMMENDED # OF SLIDES
60	÷	**3**	=	**20**

- It is recommended that you use no more than [**the calculated number**] content slides for you presentation.

NOTE: Title page slides, transition slides, and the like should not be included in this calculation. Only consider *content* slides.

15. **What supporting Communication Tools are needed for <u>each TOPIC</u> to better help inform, motivate, persuade, or demonstrate to the audience, and support the accomplishment of the purpose, goals, objectives, and desired outcomes of the presentation?**

For each TOPIC, select one or more of the following supporting Communication Tools that you plan to use.

- None needed for this topic
- Graphic
- Photograph
- Calculation or chart
- Video
- Audio
- Other

See the table below for an example.

Theme/Topic	Description	Supporting Communication Tool Needed
Seafood (Theme)		
Lobster (Topic)	I will discuss the origins of lobster as a food item; I will discuss the nutritional benefits of eating lobster; I will discuss the various types of lobster we eat most often and their typical prices; I will discuss the major sources of lobster and why they are so expensive	Photograph, Chart
Salmon (Topic)	Description	Graphic
Sea Bass (Topic)	Description	Graphic
Shrimp (topic)	Description	None needed for this Topic

This shows that the presenter will use I photograph and I chart for the "lobster" topic; I graphic for the "salmon" topic and I graphic for the "shrimp" topic, for a total of **4 additional slides**

Each Communication Tool option that is chosen (other than "None needed for this topic"), should account for one (1) slide of the total number of slides you plan to use for your presentation (from question #14).

16. **Determine the level of detail / complexity of each TOPIC by selecting an option from the list below.**

    How detailed is this TOPIC? (Select one choice for each TOPIC)

    - Complex, difficult, or hard to explain
    - Standard or medium in complexity; not difficult
    - Basic, simple, easy, not complex

    See the table below for an example.

Theme/Topic	Description	Supporting Communication Tool Needed	Level of Detail or Complexity
Seafood (Theme)			
Lobster (Topic)	I will discuss the origins of lobster as a food item; I will discuss the nutritional benefits of eating lobster; I will discuss the various types of lobster we eat most often and their typical prices; I will discuss the major sources of lobster and why they are so expensive	Photograph, Chart	Complex/Difficult
Salmon (Topic)	Description	Graphic	Standard / Medium
Sea Bass (Topic)	Description	Graphic	Standard / Medium
Shrimp (topic)	Description	None needed for this Topic	Basic/Simple

17. Using the rules table below, calculate the number of slides you <u>WOULD need</u> based on questions #15 and #16.

Rules Table for Content Slides

Criteria	Number of Slides Needed
Complex, difficult, or hard to explain	**2 or 3 Slides** Typically, three (3) slides are recommended if the total recommended number of slides (from question #14) is 20 or greater; otherwise, two (2) slides
Standard or medium in complexity; not difficult	**1 or 2 Slides** Typically, two (2) slides are recommended if the total recommended number of slides (from question #14) is 20 or greater; otherwise, one (1) slide
Basic, simple, easy, not complex	**1 Slide**
YES: Supporting communication tool(s) needed	1 slide for each communication tool needed
NO: Supporting communication tool(s) needed	**NONE**

For example:

SLIDE CALCULATION TABLE BASED ON THE RULES

TOPIC	COMPLEX, DIFFICULT, OR HARD TO EXPLAIN	STANDARD OR MEDIUM IN COMPLEXITY; NOT DIFFICULT	BASIC, SIMPLE, EASY, NOT COMPLEX	YES: SUPPORTING COMMUNICA TION TOOL(S) NEEDED	NO: SUPPORTING COMMUNICA TION TOOL(S) NEEDED	TOTALS
LOBSTER	3			2		5
SALMON		2		1		3
SEA BASS		2		1		3
SHRIMP			1		0	1
CARROTS			1		0	1
SPINACH			1		0	1
TURNIPS	3			1		4
BROCCOLI			1		0	1
CAKE			1	1		2
PIE		2			0	2
ICE CREAM			1		0	1
FRUIT		2		1		3
(A) TOTAL NUMBER OF SLIDES CALCULATED	6	8	6	7	0	27
(B) TOTAL RECOMMENDED NUMBER OF SLIDES FROM QUESTION #14						
(C) DIFFERENCE						

Caution: If the Total Number of Slides Calculated ("A" in the table on the preceding page) is greater than the Total Recommended Number of Slides ("B" in the table on the preceding page and from question #14), then you should re-evaluate which slides and how many you will need to support each TOPIC.

18. **Create your slide outline and the total number of content slides planned for this presentation based on your estimates in question #17, and add one (1) slide for the Agenda and one (1) slide for the Close.**

    See the table below for an example.

Topic—Theme Alignment

Item	Number of Slides
Agenda	1
Theme 1: Seafood	
Lobster	5
Salmon	3
Sea Bass	3
Shrimp	1
Theme 2: Vegetables	
Carrots	1
Spinach	1
Turnips	4
Broccoli	1
Theme 3: Dessert	
Cake	2
Pie	2
Ice Cream	1
Fruit	3
Close	1
TOTAL NUMBER OF PLANNED SLIDES	29

Optional: Add **transition slides** between each THEME.

NOTE: Transition slides do not count toward your content slide number since they contain no content; typically they only contain a heading or title.

At this point, you should be able to develop an outline of your presentation, including the Themes, Topics, and Sub-Topics (derived from the Descriptions). I have provided a sample below.

Sample Presentation Outline

Item	Number of Slides
Agenda	1
Seafood	
LOBSTER • Sub-Topic: I will discuss the origins of lobster as a food item • Sub-Topic: I will discuss the nutritional benefits of eating lobster • Sub Topic: I will discuss the various types of lobster we eat most often and their typical prices • Sub-Topic: I will discuss the major sources of lobster and why they are so expensive	5
SALMON • Description / Sub-Topic	3

SEA BASS • Description / Sub-Topic	**3**
SHRIMP • Description / Sub-Topic	**1**
Vegetables	
CARROTS • Description / Sub-Topic	**1**
SPINACH • Description / Sub-Topic	**1**
TURNIPS • Description / Sub-Topic	**4**
BROCCOLI • Description / Sub-Topic	**1**
Dessert	
CAKE • Description / Sub-Topic	**2**
PIE • Description / Sub-Topic	**2**
ICE CREAM • Description / Sub-Topic	**1**
FRUIT • Description / Sub-Topic	**3**
Close • Description	**1**
TOTAL NUMBER OF PLANNED SLIDES	**29**

Sample Slides From Your Outline

Sample PowerPoint or OpenOffice Impress slides for this presentation may be developed (fundamentally) as in the sample below. When your presentation is created using the *SNaP Presenter* tool, the slides are auto-created for you.

SAMPLE PRESENTATION SLIDE OUTLINE

COVER SLIDE

PRESENTATION TITLE
PRESENTER NAME
DATE

AGENDA

- SEAFOOD (THEME 1)
- VEGETABLES (THEME 2)
- DESSERT (THEME 3)

SEAFOOD

LOBSTER
  - SUB-TOPIC 1

SEAFOOD

LOBSTER
  - SUB-TOPIC 2

SEAFOOD

LOBSTER
  - [COMMUNICATION TOOL]

SEAFOOD

LOBSTER
  - SUB-TOPIC N

Reminder: If TOTAL NUMBER of PLANNED SLIDES is greater than the RECOMMENDED SLIDES from question #14, this should be a **red flag** and you should reconsider the slides needed to deliver your message within the allotted time of your presentation.

CH 10

Stage 4
Validate

The most effective presentations leave the audience with an action item, to-do, next step, or a take-away from the presentation—even if it is implied and not specifically spelled out in the presentation content. These presentations move the audience to act—even if the action is simply to feel or think differently about something.

Consider this: If you leave a presentation in the same frame of mind and feeling the same way you did when you entered the presentation, then the presentation likely had no impact and was, therefore, of little value to you. And if a presentation is of little value to the audience, then it is most likely of little value to the presenter, too.

Every presentation should answer the questions: *What do I want the audience to do after they have heard my presentation? Why should they do it? How will I motivate them to do it?* This is especially true for sales presentations or those where the presenter wants the audience to take a specific action based on the presentation.

The *validation* process establishes, confirms, and "validates" that the presentation you are developing provides specific instruction on what the audience should do, feel, think, or believe after hearing your presentation, and why they should do it.

19. **Does this presentation outline specifically state and clearly explain WHAT the audience should do after hearing your presentation?**

   - If the answer is "No," this is a **red flag** and you should include the appropriate content in your presentation.

   - Explain "WHAT" you want the audience to do. Be specific.

20. **Does this presentation outline specifically state and clearly explain WHY the audience should do what you are asking of them?**

   - If the answer is "No," this is a **red flag** and you should include the appropriate content in your presentation.

   - Explain "WHY" the audience should do what you are asking of them. Be specific.

21. **Does this presentation <u>make the case for WHY</u> the**

audience should do what you are asking of them?

- If the answer is "No," this is a **red flag** and you should include the appropriate content in your presentation.

- Explain the justification for "WHY" the audience should do what you are asking of them. Be specific.

CH 11

Stage 5
Message Delivery

Effective message delivery means that the presenter was effectively able to get the audience to absorb the key message in the content of the presentation. This is best achieved: when the presenter understands and can articulate every topic and sub-topic of his or her content; when the presenter can explain and answer questions about each topic and sub-topic in the presentation; and when the presenter can validate that each topic and sub-topic are relevant to the purpose, goals, objectives, and desired outcomes of the presentation.

This **Message Delivery** section is designed to help you ensure that your presentation messaging is relevant and effective.

For best results, **complete this section with a partner.**

22. **What is your level of understanding of each TOPIC in your presentation (select all that apply for EACH TOPIC in your presentation outline)?**

    • I can explain the origin of the this topic/content [If NOT selected, this is a **red flag**]

    • The source of this content is credible [If NOT selected, this is a **red flag**]

    • I have sufficient evidence to support this claim [If NOT selected, this is a **red flag**]

    • I can explain this topic in detail if asked [If NOT selected, this is a **red flag**]

    • I know what the topic/information means; I can interpret it. [If NOT selected, this is a **red flag**]

NOTE: All **red flags** should be resolved (or eliminated) before delivering your final presentation.

23. **[Complete this section with a partner]. What questions would you and the partner have or would you anticipate the audience having while listening to this presentation, and what are your responses?**

    • List five (5) questions that you anticipate from the audience

- Write your five (5) answers to these anticipated questions

- [**Partner**]: Is this response sufficient? [If NOT, this is a **red flag**]

24. [Complete this section with a partner]. **Content Relevance: For each TOPIC and each Sub-Topic, bullet, chart, communication tool, or <u>anything</u> that you present or show on a slide, if the audience asks "So What?" about the relevance of that item to them, what would be your response? (answer below). If you do not have a valid reason or response, consider removing the content because it is likely irrelevant.**

   - [**Partner**]: For each Topic, Sub-Topic, bullet, and Communication Tool, in the presentation, ask the presenter: "So What?"

   - [**Partner**]: Is this response sufficient? [If NOT, this is a **red flag**]

NOTE: All **red flags** should be resolved (or eliminated) before delivering your final presentation.

25. [Complete this section with a partner]. **Presentation Content Effectiveness: How confident are you that the content of your presentation and your approach for sharing it will satisfy <u>the audience's</u> purpose, goals, objectives, and desired outcome of the presentation?**

Select ONE option

- I **THINK** this content and my approach will satisfy the audience's purpose, goals, objectives, and desired outcome of the presentation [If selected, this is **a red flag**]

- I **KNOW** this content and my approach will satisfy the audience's purpose, goals, objectives, and desired outcome of the presentation

- I can **PROVE** that this content and my approach will satisfy the audience's purpose, goals, objectives, and desired outcome of the presentation

- Explain your selection, especially if the selection is KNOW or PROVE. [**Partner**: Is this explanation sufficient?]

NOTE: All **red flags** should be resolved (or eliminated) before delivering your final presentation.

26. [**Complete this section with a partner**]. **Presentation Content Effectiveness: How confident are you that the content of your presentation and your approach for sharing it will satisfy <u>your</u> purpose, goals, objectives, and desired outcome of the presentation?**

Select ONE option

- I **THINK** this content and my approach will satisfy my purpose, goals, objectives, and desired outcome of the presentation [If selected, this is **a red flag**]

- I **KNOW** this content and my approach will satisfy my purpose, goals, objectives, and desired outcome of the presentation

- I can **PROVE** that this content and my approach will satisfy my purpose, goals, objectives, and desired outcome of the presentation

- Explain your selection, especially if the selection is KNOW or PROVE. [**Partner**: Is this explanation sufficient?]

NOTE: All **red flags** should be resolved (or eliminated) before delivering your final presentation.

PART FIVE

Presentation Delivery

CH 12

Stage 6
Connecting With the Audience

Some of the most effective presentations are those in which the presenter is able to "connect" with the audience. *Connecting* with an audience involves making the audience believe that you understand where they are coming from; that you empathize with them; that you and they view the world through the same lens; that they believe and can *trust* you.

27. "Credibility" is the quality of being believable and/ or trustworthy. Have you established credibility with your audience?

- If "Yes," explain how you will or have established credibility with the audience

- If "No," Explain what you will do to establish credibility with the audience [This is a **red flag**]

28. **What in your presentation will give you the opportunity to connect with your audience emotionally? In other words, how will you show them that you can relate to their interests? Explain.**

Style Points

"Style Points" are all about the finishing touches of a presentation. After you have developed the presentation content, it is now time to begin to prepare for the actual delivery of the presentation.

Presentation delivery is the packaging that the actual presentation content is enveloped in. It's about the acceptance, the performance, the visual, the auditory, the motion, the "Q" rating.

In this section, I will share some best practices, insider information, and tasty tidbits that a presenter can use to fine-tune and improve the overall effectiveness of the presentation that he or she is delivering.

Umm ... Ya Know? ... The Service Bell

One of the most distracting things a presenter can do during a presentation is to fill his or her presentation with incessant, "umms," "ya knows," and other such interjections that convey hesitation and uncertainty. Too many such interjections and the audience start to become annoyed. And in those cases where the presenter says "umm" and "ya know" a few too many times, I have witnessed audience members ignore the presentation and start *counting* the annoyances; it eventually becomes a game for the audience. The use of these interjections is almost always subconscious on the part of the presenter. And since the presenter is mostly unaware that he or she is saying "umm" and "ya know" to the point of becoming a distraction to the audience, the presenter will simply continue to do it.

So, the way to help presenters reduce the use of "umms," "ya knows," and other such interjections is to make them *aware* that they are doing it. The simple solution that I have found for making presenters aware of their use of the distracting interjections is with the assistance of a cheap $3.99 service bell.

Here is how it works: When the presenter is practicing his or her presentation, the presenter should enlist the assistance of a partner. The presenter will give the bell to the assistant and instruct the assistant to ring the bell every time the presenter says, "umm," "ya know," "like," "so," "actually," "I'm so great," or whatever repetitive annoyance the presenter utters too frequently while presenting. When the presenter launches into his or her presentation, the assistant will ring the bell and count each time the presenter says the targeted word or words. After the presenter finishes the practice round of the presentation, the assistant will inform the presenter of the number of times the annoying words were uttered.

This approach accomplishes the desired result of reducing the number of times the presenter repeats an interjection in two ways:

1. Each time the assistant rings the bell, the presenter will immediately be made aware that he or she has said a word or phrase that he or she is trying to avoid saying; this will not only drive awareness, but will also annoy the presenter into becoming more cognizant of saying the word or phrase. Over time, the presenter will become conditioned to associating the use of the word or phrase with discomfort and will reduce the use of the interjections.

2. After each practice run of the presentation, the presenter's assistant will tally up the number of times the presenter utters an undesirable interjection and share this number with the presenter. After each subsequent practice run of the presentation, the assistant will do the same. My experience has shown that, over time, the presenter will use such words less and less with each run through of the presentation. Counting the number of times each interjection is used enables the presenter and the assistant to validate this improvement.

The Stump Session

A *Stump Session* is an activity that my colleagues and I use as we prepare for our presentations. During a stump session, the presenter will deliver a practice run of the presentation and the assistants will do their best to *stump* the presenter—throwing a curve ball at the presenter in an effort to make the presenter look unprepared and throw him or her off their game.

For instance, these are the types of thing we will bring to the table during a typical stump session:

- We will think of the most relevantly-imaginative, difficult, relevantly-bizarre, and deal-breaker questions that an audience could possibly ask about the presenter's content, topic of discussion, sources of information, clothing, or anything else in an effort to stump the presenter. By doing this, the presenter will be as prepared as possible for any curve ball that can be thrown during the presentation.

- We will think of the questions that the presenter hopes no one asks during the presentation. We will analyze every single bullet point, sentence, formula, quote, image, reference, number, and assumption that the presenter says or shows during the presentation. If the presenter cannot sufficiently address our concern or answer our questions, the presenter's credibility will be impacted.

   This activity forces the presenter to "Know of what you speak or show, or don't" (either know the details of everything you present to an audience or show on a slide, or don't present it).

- Each of us will come up with three reasons why the presentation could miss the mark and not deliver on the goal, objective, or desired outcome of the presentation. This will force the presenter to determine ways to forestall or prevent this prior to the actual presentation.

The stump session activity helps the presenter better prepare for the presentation and decreases the odds that something could happen during the presentation that will negatively impact the presentation, put the presenter in an awkward position, and throw the presenter off his or her game.

The Expert Audience

When preparing for and giving a presentation, I ALWAYS assume that everyone in the audience knows at least as much as I do about the topic of my presentation or is more knowledgeable about the topic.

Consider: If you knew that you would be presenting to an audience that knows more than you do about *your* topic of discussion, how would you approach the presentation? How would you prepare differently?

Look Smart, Flip Chart

End clients, customers, presentation participants, and sales research have confirmed that presenters who can pitch on the fly (jump into an impromptu presentation on a given topic) using a whiteboard or flip charts as their medium appear more expert than presenters who only use PowerPoint slides or their equivalent.

When a presenter can walk up to a whiteboard or flip-chart and lead a discussion, this skill translates into credibility for the presenter because it makes the presenter appear as a fearless, knowledgeable authority who has done this many times before.

Incorporating the use of a whiteboard or flipchart into a presentation can pay dividends in a presentation where skill, experience, and knowledge are important attributes in a presenter to an audience.

Handling the Rude Questioner or the "Plant"

Sometimes during a presentation, an audience member will ask an off-topic, irrelevant, or challenging question—and will continue badgering the presenter about the question even after the presenter has attempted to provide an answer to the question. To make matters worse, some companies will send their own employees as "plants" at a competitor's presentation just to make the presenter and his or her company look bad. When either of these scenarios occurs, they can be difficult to handle. And if they are not handled skillfully, they can make the presenter look flustered as though he or she has lost control of the presentation.

Following is a best practice for handling these types of questioners during a presentation:

- First, answer the person's question and validate that the question has been satisfactorily answered.

- If the questioner is unsatisfied with the response and

continues to press the issue, politely attempt to answer the question a second time.

- If the questioner continues to press the issue, the presenter should say something like this: "I'm sorry that I haven't answered your question in a manner that is satisfactory to you. In the interest of time and to ensure that I can provide the other participants with the information they are here to receive from me, let's spend a few minutes after the presentation and I will address your question then. If necessary, we can exchange contact information and I will make sure that you get the information you need." And then move on with the presentation.

- If the person *still* continues to press the issue at that point, then ignore the person; he or she will begin to be seen as a disruption and the audience will ignore them.

This same process can be followed with audience members who disagree with you on certain points and it can be used to get you back on-track when an audience member or circumstances take you off-track.

Short Practice Makes Better

It is very easy for people to become better presenters through frequent practice. It is not necessary to develop a long, complex presentation just to practice with; a simple five-minute practice presentation will do the job just fine.

Here is what you can do:

- For your practice presentation, pick a topic that you

know inside-and-out. For example, if you are a parent, you can choose to do a five-to-ten-minute presentation on something interesting about your kids. If you are a Human Resources professional, you can do a presentation on the most unusual job interviews you have conducted. And if you enjoy playing golf, you can do a presentation on your best golf game. Whatever your chosen topic, just make sure it is something that you can talk about without any thought and that you enjoy talking about.

In order to become a better presenter, it is not necessary to create a difficult presentation to practice with. The easiest presentations are the best to use because, while delivering the presentation, you don't have to think about your content and, therefore, can focus on perfecting other things such as hand gestures, vocal inflection, eye contact, and other contributors to effective presentation delivery.

- Deliver on-the-spot and pop-presentations on the fly. Here is how to do it: ask a friend or relative to—unannounced—ask you to do a two-minute presentation on-the-spot on a topic of something found in the immediate surroundings where you are standing. So, as you walk around the house, office, shopping mall, or backyard, you could be asked at any moment to give an impromptu presentation.

If, for example, you and a friend are at a supermarket in the vegetable aisle, your friend will say, "Give me a two minute presentation on carrots," and you will launch into your presentation on carrots—right there in the vegetable aisle. This is not only a good way to sharpen your presentation delivery skills in a stressful environment (the thought of doing a presentation in the vegetable aisle of a supermarket in front of total strangers who will think you are crazy can be stress-inducing), but is also a good way to get used to presenting under stress.

Audio-Visual Reminders

Many years ago while I was working as a consultant for a major technology company, I was asked by one of the company's executives to deliver a presentation on the status of a global initiative on which I was working. I arrived at the facility and was taken to the conference room. An administrator came into the room and said that the executive and his team would be there in fifteen minutes and that I should go ahead and set up for my presentation.

I opened my laptop PC, opened my PowerPoint presentation, and waked over to the projector to connect the PC. To my surprise, the projector's bulb was blown and I couldn't show my presentation slides! Fortunately, there were still ten minutes before the executive and his team were to come to the conference room. So I bolted from the room, asked the administrator to call the audio-visual (A/V) person ASAP to bring another projector AND a spare bulb to the executive conference room.

Not knowing how long this would take, I returned to the conference room and scoured the room for a back-up projector bulb. Having delivered many presentations over the years, I knew that some of the older projector models housed back-up bulbs inside the machine itself. So I opened the projector and—to my pleasant surprise—

there was a spare bulb! I installed the bulb, hooked-up my laptop PC, and—two minutes later—the executive and his team arrived. No, the audio-visual person never showed up.

As it turned out, the executive purposefully removed the bulb from the projector as a test to see how resourceful I could be and to see how I would have handled the situation if I wasn't able to locate the spare bulb.

This incident taught me a valuable lesson about delivering presentations with the use of audio-visual equipment: be prepared for the possibility that the different A/V platforms you elect to use as part of your presentation are inadequate, unavailable, or fail mid-way through your presentation.

Here are some things to consider:

- If you use a microphone, do a sound-check to ensure the proper volume and sound levels. Make sure there is a back-up microphone (handheld or clip-on) available.

- If you use a projector to transmit your slides, make sure there is a back-up bulb and projector available. Make sure there is a back-up PC with your presentation's program available (e.g. Microsoft PowerPoint, Adobe Acrobat, etc.).

- Create a back-up plan for the possibility that your microphone, projector, PC, flipchart, whiteboard, and handouts are unavailable when you begin your presentation.

CH 13

Presentation Slides: Best Practices

When giving a slide presentation (a presentation in which the presenter uses PowerPoint slides, transparencies, or their equivalent) far too many presenters make the mistake of thinking that the fancier and photo-filled their slides, the better will be their presentations. This is not correct. Overly complex, busy, or cluttered slides move the audience's focus away from the presenter and onto the fancy slides. And when that happens, the audience is not listening to your message which will reduce the overall effectiveness of the presentation.

I once had a colleague who bragged about how he could make PowerPoint slides "sing!" My reply was: "I'm just the opposite. I want my slides to be mute so that the audience will pay attention to *me*. That way, there's only one person trying to communicate the presentation's message."

Presentation slides should be the Robin to your Batman: they should assist you when needed, but otherwise sit in the background unobtrusively.

Presentation slides can be a great complement to a presentation if used wisely. Following are some best practices for creating and using presentation slides to enhance your presentations.

Batman and Robin

The role of presentation slides should be to support, not dominate, a presenter's message. From the audience perspective, slides should be used as a guide for the audience to follow your message. From the presenter's perspective, slides should be used as a guide for the presenter (they help the presenter keep his or her place in the presentation and stay on-message) and as supporting tools to help embellish a message.

Think of Batman and Robin. Batman is the lead crime fighter in the duo; it is *his* show. He is the focus of the story. Every now-and-then, just to add some spice to a situation, Batman's sidekick, Robin, is given a role to enhance the situation in the story. Then, after Robin has served his purpose, he is relegated to background status again.

Imagine if one story in the series depicted *Robin* as the lead character (yes, Robin who doesn't know how to lead an investigation) and Batman as his sidekick (yes, Batman who is really the main character with all of the knowledge and leadership). The show would seem really weird, wouldn't it? People tuning in to see their hero, Batman, rid Gotham City of crime would be truly disappointed. Robin's role, they would argue, is to *support* batman, NOT take over for him! This same logic holds true for presentation slides: they should support a presenter, not overshadow, detract from, or take over for her.

The K.E.N. Principle™: Keep 'em Naked

Presentation slides should do their job and nothing more. They should pop-up on the screen, deliver their message as succinctly as possible, and then shut up.

The problem with fancy, overly-populated slides is that they never *shut up*; they keep "talking" while the presenter is also trying to talk. And one of the inhibitors to effective communication is two people "talking" at the same time. When both the slides and the presenter are talking simultaneously, half of the audience will be listening to the slides and half of the audience will be listening to the presenter. When this happens, the presenter loses half of his or her audience.

One of the easiest things a presenter can do to avoid this problem is to create PowerPoint (or equivalent) slides that succinctly says what they need to say and then shuts up. And the way to create these obedient, supporting slides is to follow my K.E.N. Principle™ and *Keep 'em Naked*.

"Naked" slides are slides that are as sparse as they can possibly be while still conveying the message that the presenter intends for the slides to convey. Slides shouldn't tell the *whole* story (the slides will be too busy and distracting), but each slide should provide a *part* of the narrative of the story that the audience can digest in **ten (10) seconds or less**.

For example, if I had four minutes or less to present an overview of the rare Vancouver Island Marmot and I decided to use presentation slides, I would create two slides: one to provide an overview of the animal and one to show a picture or photograph of what the animal looks like (see my slide samples below).

NAKED SLIDE SAMPLE

The Vancouver Island Marmot

+ Habitat: Vancouver Island, in B.c.
+ 1998: All-time low of 75
+ Listed as endangered in May 2000
+ Goal: sustainable population of 400-600 in the wild

The text slide will be kept naked, and I would present the data on the naked slide using ***progressive disclosure***—a technique of showing one line of text at a time as I describe it. And when I show the photograph, I will shut up, let the audience absorb the image, and when I believe they have done so, I will remove the image from the screen to have the audience re-focus on me.

Be careful showing pictures or photographs during a presentation. Pictures and photographs—more than anything else in a slide deck—will steal the audience's attention totally away from the presenter. So, if you decide to use a picture or photograph as part of your presentation (as I did in the example above) use it purposefully by showing it, shutting up while it's on the screen (so that the audience can appreciate the image as you intend), and once done, immediately remove the slide from the screen in order to regain the audience's attention.

Storyboard

A storyboard is a visual representation of the presentation's content. Creating a storyboard will help you plan your presentation visuals slide-by-slide.

When I develop presentations that use supporting slides, I grab a pencil and some paper and I begin to plan out what the supporting presentation slides will look like, what information they will contain, and how many slides I will need in order to convey a message; this is an example of storyboarding. Storyboarding saves time and makes it easier to design your slides prior to creating the final slides in PowerPoint, Impress, or other tools.

FROM STORYBOARD TO SLIDES

STORYBOARD

What We Do
. Sales
. Training
- Strategy
` Consulting

SLIDES

PROFANITY

WHAT WE DO

+ SALES
+ TRAINING
+ STRATEGY
+ CONSULTING

PART SIX

Fine-Tuning

CH 14

Fine-Tuning Checklist

From the table below, **select (✔) each item that you have completed or made a decision about.** If you have not completed an item or made a decision about what you will do for an item, this is a **red flag.**

This double-check checklist contains a list of items that most people skim over and do not pay enough attention to as they prepare for their presentations. Simply remembering to pay attention to and account for these activities can help presenters significantly improve their presentation effectiveness.

✔	Category	Style Points
	Strategy	A *strategy* is a plan of action for how you will accomplish an objective. What is your presentation strategy? How will you accomplish your goals, objectives, and desired outcome of the presentation? How will you present your position? The *how* you present your position is often more important than the position itself.
	Attire	Overdress one notch up. For instance, if the attire is "business casual" wear full business dress. If it is casual, wear "business casual." Use your judgment as to what is appropriate based on the event.
	Attire	Do not distract. Find the balance between dressing appropriately, professionally, and "stylishly"—while not wearing anything that distracts the audience from paying attention to your message delivery.
	Media	How large is the venue in which the presentation will be held? Will you need a microphone? If so, which will you use: clip on or hand-held? Will one be available?
	Media	If using audio or video to support your presentation, will you have an opportunity to test them prior to the start of the presentation? What is your backup plan if the technology fails of becomes unavailable?
	Rehearse	Eye contact. Engage the audience by acknowledging the entire audience/room with your focus and eye contact. Pay attention to each quadrant of the room. Truly look at people and not simply glance at them in passing.

Rehearse	"Bell" Ringing. Using a bell, buzzer, or something that makes an annoying sound on-demand—along with using a partner or audience—rehearse your presentation. Each time you say "Umm," "you know," or some other annoyance, have the partner ring the bell, buzzer, or simply say "Stop!" each time you say one of those words; track the number of times you say them. This will help make you cognizant of saying the words and, ultimately, help you reduce their utterance.
Rehearse	Your hands. If you cannot decide what to do with your hands, try rehearsing while folding them or clasping them at your belly button or above your beltline.
Rehearse	Know your content. When you know your content and what you are going to say, you can focus on your style and delivery.
Opening	Rehearse your opening and the transition into your content. The opening will often set the audience's expectation of the presentation and you as a presenter.
Opening	Humor. Do **NOT** open your presentation with a joke. Joke-telling during a presentation is risky. Avoid it at all costs unless you are presenting to your family.
Opening	Break the ice, calm your nerves, and engage your audience by asking a general, relevant, interesting question up front—the answer to which will smoothly lead you into your presentation.
Opening	Ease into your presentation by sharing an interesting anecdote related to your overall presentation title / topic.

	Opening	Explain why your audience should care to listen to what you are about to present.
	Opening	Credibility. Modestly share your relevant background, credentials, and experience with the audience up front. This answers the question: "Why should I listen to *you*?"
	Q&A	If you don't know the answer to a question, admit it. It is important to anticipate all of the possible (significant) questions that can be asked during your presentation and prepare an answer for each.
	Surprise!	What would you do if an audience member yelled, "You're full of @#&*!" during your presentation? Or yelled, "What you are saying is not correct!" What if someone walked out mid-presentation? Prepare for these outside possibilities so that if one should happen, it will not sink your presentation.

Conclusion

For me, becoming a better presenter is about constant learning and incremental improvement. Call me strange, but I enjoy watching awful infomercials. Why? Because infomercials are often hosted by pitchmen and women who are effective communicators, and I find that watching good presenters in action is enjoyable to me. In addition, I might even pick-up a useful idea while I'm being entertained.

My presentation effectiveness learning doesn't begin or end with watching awful infomercials, however. My learning and study go back as far as Abraham Lincoln, who would engage every member of his audience by making genuine eye contact and speaking directly to people. He would also point directly at audience members and address them by name or description regardless of where they were sitting in the room (e.g. "From the woman sitting right here in the blue dress, to you, the man sitting in the back corner of the room wearing the green scarf …").

And in more recent times, wonderful orators like author James Baldwin and former President John F. Kennedy offer great insight into being a great presenter. Whether it is James Baldwin's excellent combination of smooth, meaningful gesturing and vocal variety, and his debate-like preparedness and delivery, or Jack Kennedy's combination of confidence, power, timing, and natural humor, I use every opportunity available to learn to become a better presenter.

These great presenters were more than just a combination of personality and delivery style. They were also masters of *content* development and inclusion.

As I hope you have come to appreciate after reading this book, becoming a better or great presenter begins with great *content*. That content should support the goals, objectives, and desired outcomes of the presentation from both the audience and presenter perspectives. And the presenter who can marry great content with credibility, a connection with the audience, and solid delivery skills will most assuredly deliver outstanding presentations.

The Presentation Impact Grid™ below depicts the findings of presentation effectiveness research that I conducted over a four-year period. The findings are based on a combination of user feedback surveys, audience feedback interview sessions, client feedback, presenter input, and marketing effectiveness study. The grid shows the relationships between:

- *Presentation* **Effectiveness** and various attributes
- *Presenter* **Effectiveness** and various attributes

It depicts the level of impact (high impact or low impact) that each of the listed attributes can have on the overall effectiveness of a presentation or the effectiveness of the presenter. For instance, an attribute such as presentation content can impact both the effectiveness of the presenter and the presentation. In the grid, this is highlighted by the start in the upper-right quadrant.

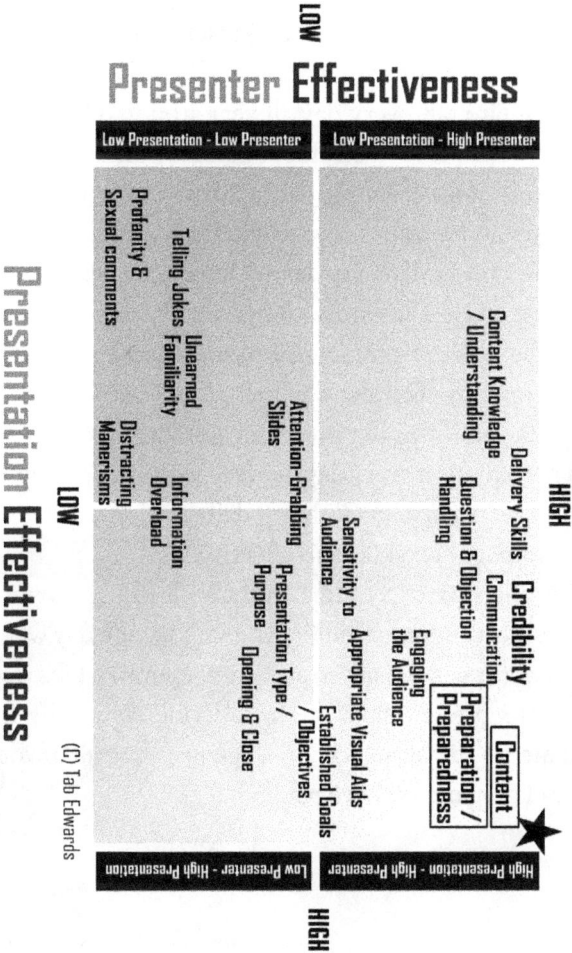

The Presentation Impact Grid (PIG)™

Presenter Effectiveness

LOW

HIGH

Low Presentation - Low Presenter	Low Presentation - High Presenter
Profanity & Sexual comments	Content Knowledge / Understanding
Unearned Familiarity	Delivery Skills **Credibility**
Telling Jokes	Question & Objection Handling Communication
Attention-Grabbing Slides	Engaging the Audience
Distracting Mannerisms	Sensitivity to Appropriate Visual Aids Audience
Information Overload	Presentation Type / Established Goals
	Purpose Opening & Close / Objectives
	Content **Preparation / Preparedness**

| Low Presenter - High Presentation | High Presentation - High Presenter |

Presentation Effectiveness

LOW

HIGH

(C) Tab Edwards

As the Presentation Impact Grid™ shows, presentation content and the presenter's degree of preparedness are two of the most important determinants of good, effective presentations.

Becoming a better presenter is just like becoming better at any other endeavor: it takes practice. Great athletes practice their craft every day all year around. Great musicians practice their instrument several hours each day. Great chefs cook every day and experiment with different flavors and cuisines. Great writers conduct research and write constantly in order to hone their craft. And great presenters? They are no different. One cannot hope to become a better presenter if one does not work at it more frequently than the day before they are to deliver a presentation. Even if a presenter does not have to deliver a presentation every day or every week, the presenter should at least *think about* things daily that he or she can do to improve their skills and effectiveness.

Through practice and continued learning, anyone can become a better presenter. And on that one day when a customer, peer, or other audience member tells you that, "Your presentation was wonderful! You truly inspired me," it will be an acknowledgement that all of your work and preparation have paid off.

About the Author

Tab Edwards is the author of seven books and is widely considered to be one of the most effective, engaging, and entertaining public speakers and presenters throughout the country. He has trained, coached, developed, and mentored thousands of professionals around the world to become more effective public speakers and skilled presenters; he also coaches Toastmasters members to help them hone their skills and improve their performance.

His Presentation Skills Improvement workshops, coaching sessions, and seminars are highly regarded, and have been provided to professionals at companies around the world, including IBM Corporation, AT&T, Pfizer, Staples, and Citigroup to name a few.

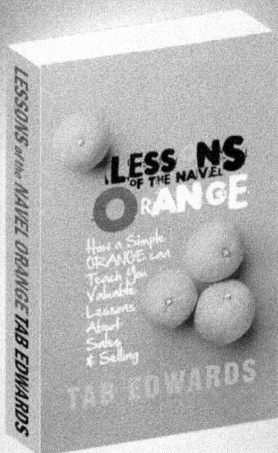

Index

C

Y

Ya Know 132

Z

Zoot suits 52
   Pimp convention 52